Best Wishes

John Greig,

Rangers FC

A Captain's Part

JOHN GREIG

A Captain's Part

FOREWORD BY DAVIE WHITE

STANLEY PAUL *London*

STANLEY PAUL & CO LTD
178–202 Great Portland Street, London, W.1

AN IMPRINT OF THE HUTCHINSON GROUP

London Melbourne Sydney
Auckland Bombay Toronto
Johannesburg New York

First published 1968

© John Greig 1968

*This book has been set in Baskerville, printed
and bound in Great Britain on Antique Wove
paper by The Garden City Press Limited
Letchworth, Hertfordshire*
09 089250 X

CONTENTS

ILLUSTRATIONS

Foreword
by Davie White

VERY OFTEN the most important decision the manager of a club has to make is the choice of player to be captain of his team.

When I took over the managership of Rangers last season I did not have that decision to make; it had already been made for me by the previous manager Scot Symon. And his choice of John Greig as skipper was exactly the one I would have made myself.

John has the outstanding attributes that you look for in the man who is to be captain of a team. He has the personal drive and powerful personality that every leader has to have. He has the respect of his fellow players, something that is essential if a team skipper is to carry authority on to the field. And he has the ability to read the way a game is going and make any alterations he might think necessary in the formation during a match without constantly having to look to the dug-out for guidance.

As well as that, of course, a captain has to be the man who can interpret his manager's ideas and help to get them over to the other players. John Greig has all these qualities and more.

For instance, I always feel that a captain must be able to put worries about his own form out of his mind and think, very often, of the team first. He must put the team before his own personal problems. John can do this.

When he has a bad game he doesn't retreat into himself. He still maintains the role of captain, the job of keeping everyone else on their toes.

What I'm saying is this—John can have a bad game yet still come into the dressing room and give other players 'stick' if their performances haven't been up to standard. He is honest enough to admit that he has played badly himself and yet by his strength of character, by his personality, he can still give another player a few words and get away with it. That he does this is testimony to the respect his team-mates have for his opinions and his ability.

Nor is John a *prima donna*. He is captain of Rangers, captain of Scotland and yet there is no sign of big-headedness.

When I first took over people in the game warned me that I might get a bit of trouble from the big-name players, the established stars. It was clear that the players they meant were John, Ronnie McKinnon and Willie Henderson, the established international players. Yet, since I became manager I have had nothing but co-operation from all three. These three, and John, in particular, as skipper, helped ease things for me when I took over in November. There were no snags, no problems, no difficulties, because John led the co-operation between the players and myself in the dressing-room.

I was a team captain myself at Clyde for six years before I became manager at Shawfield. And in my own experience I feel that a captain and a manager must build a special understanding about the game. I did this with John Prentice and now I think I am doing it from the other side—the manager's side—with John.

Referring to John Prentice, brings me to another point about John Greig's ability as a captain. He has been chosen as skipper by no fewer than *six* managers. At Ibrox by Scot Symon and myself and for Scotland by Celtic manager Jock Stein, in his term as Scotland team manager, by John Prentice, by Malcolm Macdonald and by the present team manager Bobby Brown. All of us have recognised the qualities of leadership that John Greig has.

He gives everything for his team; he will play in any position he is asked to fill and always he will be an inspiration to his team-mates.

Off the field, too, he is the perfect ambassador for his club and for his country. When he was named Player of the Year by the Scottish Football Writers' Association two years ago it was an honour that no one would have argued about.

John Greig deserved it. John Greig earned it . . . just as he has earned the captaincy of Rangers and of Scotland.

D.W.

I

Captain for the first time

WHEN I WAS asked to be captain of Scotland for the first
time I thought that it was in the nature of a stop-gap appointment, and that I would be replaced by one of the better-
known Scots' stars for the very next game. It never happened,
however, and I'm still Scotland's captain today. But, then, it
was so different. I was asked to captain my country by Celtic
boss Jock Stein who was then Scottish team manager, during
the time we played our last World Cup qualifying game
against Italy in Naples in 1965. And I was asked at a time
when the Scottish team was going into a match without two
men who had skippered Scotland when I was in the team,
Billy McNeill and Jim Baxter. We were also without Denis
Law, another former Scotland captain.

So, Jock Stein came and asked me to take over the job.
I did. And then afterwards, when we had lost 3–0 and failed
to make the 1966 Finals in England, I thought that was that.
I had done the job that every kid who kicks a ball dreams
about. I had captained my country and though it might

never happen again, no one could take that away from me.
I really believed that I had been 'captain for a day'....

There was a gap then in between our international games
and the next time we played was five months later when we
met England at Hampden. And I was named captain again
by the new team manager John Prentice. I have been captain
in all the games I've played for my country since.

Of course, in these games the big name players have been
back in the side. Jim Baxter and Denis Law, for instance,
both £100,000 players. I wondered at the start how I would
react to being their onfield boss, so to speak; me, a one-club
man, who has been with Rangers since I first moved into
senior football.

Even now people ask me if I do find it difficult, if Jim and
Denis are big-headed, if they big-time the rest of the lads.
To me they are the same as any other member of the international team. If I have to say anything to them on the field
during a game in my job as captain they accept it. They do
not tell me to 'get lost' or anything like that. They react the
same as their team-mates. They listen and then they give me
an answer. For instance, if I have to ask one of them why
they are not sticking to the tactics which were laid down by
the team manager before the game, they will give me reasons
for it. Jim might say he is trying to get away from someone
who is trying to mark him out of the game. Denis might be
playing a little deeper for the same reason. You can accept
their views or insist they should stick to the plans. Whatever
happens, they will listen to you.

Mind you, the role of captain in Scotland's team does not
carry the same responsibility as it does with a club team. With
Rangers if special circumstances come up I can change the
team around on the field. I've done it several times when
things started to go wrong. I have made a change, perhaps
because of a minor injury which cannot be seen from the

trainer's bench, and then explained it to the manager afterwards.

At Scotland level, however, that responsibility is not placed
on the captain. If it was at any time, mind you, I'm quite
sure that the big-name players in the Scottish team would
accept the captain's orders, whether it was me or anyone else.
They would do it because they are professionals and in our
highly professional game you learn to take orders when they
are given on the field.

I enjoy being captain and I am happy that that day in
Naples Jock Stein gave me the chance to do the job. Yet, it
was the Celtic boss who gave me the biggest problem of my
whole career. Again it was against Italy in a World Cup
qualifying game. Again he asked me to do a special job for
him.

This was the game at Hampden a few months before we
travelled to Naples and Stein, made team manager for our
World Cup bid, asked me if I would play at right-back. He
needed someone for that position and he needed someone
who would overlap for him. He wanted this because he knew
that the Italians would play the game very tight at Hampden.
He knew they would come to Hampden looking for a draw
and he wanted to offset these tactics. He succeeded in exactly
the way he wanted, with me breaking through down the right
and scoring in the last minute of the match. That goal kept
our hopes alive until Naples but at the same time it could
have finished my international career.

After that game everyone got it into their heads that I was
a full-back . . . everyone except me. Jock Stein kept me
there in a match against Wales. John Prentice, in his spell as
manager, also kept me there. And so did Kilmarnock manager
Malcolm Macdonald when he took over as team manager for
several games.

I was still playing my usual double centre-half role with

Rangers, sticking in the middle of the defence around Ronnie
McKinnon. With Scotland, though, I was at right-back and
I didn't like the position at all. I did not have the experience
for this role. I kept finding myself on the wrong side of
wingers; I did not seem to position myself properly. For a
time I thought I was certain to lose my place in the Scotland
team. Then, suddenly, I was moved back to the position I felt
I could play best, alongside Ronnie McKinnon.

Mind you this is not always the job I get in the Rangers or
Scotland team. Last season I was being used as a link man
both with Rangers and with Scotland. I enjoyed that, in fact
I prefer to play there, even though I feel I am better in a
defensive role.

The snag about playing around the centre-half is that you
are never enough in the game. There are spells of inactivity
when you are deep in defence and I detest that. I prefer to
be in the thick of things all the time and when former
Rangers' manager Scot Symon moved me up to become link
man last year in a Fairs Cup game at Ibrox against Dynamo
Dresden I was much happier. This is a harder job, however,
as I am up and down the field, attacking and defending,
working all the time, involved in the game all the time. That's
the way I like it to be for the other position leaves me with
less work to do.

I realise, however, that playing as a double centre-half is
probably my best position. For one thing, I've been playing
there longer, and for most of the time I've been in that job
I've been working with Ronnie McKinnon at club and international level. We have worked out an understanding between
us and I know the way he likes me to play when I am beside
him. Of course certain actions start to come quite naturally
to you when you've played together for a long spell. You know
instinctively which one of you is going to go for a certain ball,

A great night for John Greig when the Scottish Football
Writers Association named him as their Player of the Year in 1966

The England team celebrate after their World Cup victory.
From left to right: Nobby Stiles, Bobby Moore, Geoff Hurst and
Martin Peters

Geoff Hurst scores England's fourth goal in the World Cup final
against West Germany

England World Cup player Bobby Charlton fails to beat the Russian goalkeeper in a match against Russia in 1967

Nobby Stiles and Alan Ball, both World Cup players, seen together before the start of an Everton *v* Manchester United match

Scotland 'keeper Bobby Ferguson is beaten by a shot from a
Brazilian forward in the 1-1 draw at Hampden while skipper
John Greig just fails to get in his tackle

The world's greatest player Pele after an incident with Billy
Bremner. Pele is on the ground while Bremner is held off by
another Brazilian. Greig has his back to the camera

or which one of you is going to tackle a specific player as he comes through.

The main quality required for the double centre-half role is the ability to read the game. At Ibrox Dave Smith has been doing that job while I've been in midfield and he has that ability. Yet with Scotland Bobby Brown, the team manager, often feels that I am best back there alongside Ronnie McKinnon. I never argue with any decision a manager makes about where I play. I will play in any position and I will do exactly what the manager thinks is best for the team. Several times last season when we had injury problems I reverted to full-back for Rangers.

I accept all this just as I accepted the full-back position for Scotland when Jock Stein told me it was going to be best for the team. It was that night and that proved to me that no matter what you want yourself the needs of the team must come first. If I am wanted as a full-back, as a link man or as a double centre-half I'll get on with it. But goals or no goals, I know that I will never be a top-class full back. . . .

2

England's World Cup win

IN SCOTLAND many people refused to be too impressed by the England World Cup win in the summer of 1966. I felt a bit that way myself but it wasn't through any personal jealousy ... though we all felt rather sick in the Scotland team when we were knocked out by Italy in Naples.

However, that didn't affect my thinking. I honestly did not feel that England were the best team in the tournament. They were not at that time, and still are not today, an attractive team to watch and that alone makes it difficult for Scottish fans to accept them as champions of the world. In Scotland the traditional heroes of the game are the gifted ball players. There were few of these in England's team....

People in Scotland don't want to watch dull, 'method' football. They still thrill most at individual brilliance and the only man who gave them that in the England team was Bobby Charlton. Then again, the 4–3–3 set-up evolved by Sir Alf Ramsey left the English team without wingers, another blow to Scots' fans who admire wing play so much. To them it was not the way the game was meant to be played. They still felt that the game should be entertaining, alive, instead of methodical and defensive.

Before the World Cup I felt the same way about tactics; in certain ways I still do, but I also realise that Sir Alf went for these methods because he felt they suited the players he had at his disposal. I think he would have used wingers if he believed that the wing men he had at his disposal would have done better for him than the players he decided eventually to stick by.

Sir Alf tried Peter Thompson and Ian Callaghan of Liverpool, Terry Paine of Southampton, and John Connelly, then of Manchester United, before finally deciding that the 4–3–3 pattern was the one that would win the World Cup, a victory he had always claimed England could achieve. In that sense, then, Ramsey deserved every possible praise for achieving what he set out to do. Yet that does not mean that his ideas and his tactics must forever remain above criticism.

The full impact of the dull, efficient and often downright negative tactics that England used will not be seen until the next World Cup in Mexico in 1970. We may get hints before that, but for the full effect we must wait until Mexico. Then we will find out if the safety-first techniques of Ramsey are to replace the flowing football that many other countries have tried to give to the world.

Before England took the world crown in 1966, the Brazilians had reigned as champions for the two previous tournaments, in Sweden in 1958 and in Chile in 1962. They helped give the 4–2–4 set-up to football and also provided the game with some of its greatest individualists. They proved that individual genius could win the top honours in football. They did that by winning two World Cups with stars such as Djalma Santos, Zito, Didi, Pele and Garrincha. Their brilliance, their flair, their unmatched talents captured the imaginations of football lovers everywhere. Not even Sir Alf can claim that his England team has done that!

Sure, Brazil relied on some method, but never the method of Ramsey. The Brazilians allowed Pele and Garrincha to develop into stars, stars who attracted the fans to football, stars who meant glamour and entertainment and excitement. England don't set out to entertain . . . they simply set out to win. That is why we must assess Ramsey's victory again when 1970 comes around. . . .

For other countries may decide to follow England's lead. Brazil, defeated in their section games in England, have already stated that they want to make their game more physical, more methodical; to follow the successful teams in Europe. If they do and other talented Latin countries follow them then football will suffer and England will not escape the blame!

I would have preferred to see Hungary or Portugal win the 1966 World Cup, especially the Hungarians. Both teams played open, attractive football and they both had stars that people wanted to watch, Eusebio, who scored so many goals for Portugal, and Albert and Farkas for Hungary, players who delighted the whole country with their display against the Brazilians at Goodison Park.

But, of course, Portugal went out to England—a method team—in the semi-finals, and Hungary went out to Russia —another method team—in the quarter-finals. Method won in each case while individual brilliance was defeated and so in Mexico in 1970 we could well see the dullest World Cup in history.

If you happen to think that I'm exaggerating the situation just take a look at what went on in European football when Inter-Milan reigned as European Cup holders. Their success, based on Helenio Herrera's *cattanacio*, the most defensive system I've ever come up against, resulted in clubs everywhere trying to copy them. They influenced the whole of Italy and the whole Continent of Europe during their spell as champions, a spell that was ended by Celtic's victory in Lisbon, a victory for attacking football, remember.

I think the England success can have the same effect on world football, epecially when you remember that the Russians are also being very successful. They are, in fact, even worse to watch in action than England! Apart from the bright attacking bursts of Chislenko they are rarely inspired. They are competent, workmanlike, efficient and boring. When they drew 2–2 at Wembley against England last year it must have been as exciting to watch as a chess game . . . two teams dedicated to defence, two teams determined to give nothing away.

Still, though I've had my say, and I'm saying it after beating the world champions on their home ground, I doubt if any criticism of mine will affect Sir Alf Ramsey. He has already shown that his feelings about Scotland and the Scottish game are not exactly complimentary. He's shown that by his comments after almost every representative game between the two countries. He seems to look on us as second-raters, from a second-class soccer country. Certainly he does not rate us with his own players, the players he reckons are masters of the world!

Yet, if it was not for players from all over Britain how would English club football look? Would it be as highly thought of as it is at the moment? I doubt it. Take Tommy Lawrence, Ronnie Yeats and Ian St John away from Liverpool; take Tony Dunne, Pat Crerand, Denis Law and George Best away from Manchester United; take Gary Sprake, Billy Bremner and Johnny Giles away from Leeds United; take Mike England, Alan Gilzean and Jimmy Robertson away from Spurs; take Eddie McCreadie and Charlie Cooke away from Chelsea. The list you can make up that way is almost endless and it has been that way for a long, long time. English players are no better than players from Scotland, Ireland or Wales. Their

national team simply has more opportunities to get together
before games. They are released when Sir Alf Ramsey wants
them . . . the other home countries do not get that privilege.

Just thinking along these lines, for a moment, here is a
team I would like to play in against England, a team made
up of the rest of Britain, a team that would beat the English
even more decisively than Scotland have beaten them. I've
put myself in, because it's a game I would hate to miss if it
ever came off. Anyhow, here is the team—Sprake (Wales);
Greig (Scotland), Hennessey (Wales), England (Wales),
McCreadie (Scotland); Bremner (Scotland), Law (Scotland);
Johnstone or Henderson (both Scotland), W. Davies (Wales),
Dougan (Ireland) and Best (Ireland).

.Anyway, that's only a dream, but it's a dream that would
turn out a nightmare for Sir Alf and his men. I'm sure of
that.

Just as sure as I was when we beat England in the April
following their World Cup victory. There are times when you
get a feeling before a game that you are going to win . . . that
was one of these times. I've never known a Scottish team so
confident, especially when the odds seemed to be stacked so
highly against them. Maybe, that's what helped us, that and
all the suggestions that came from the English newspapers
that we should not be allowed on the same field as the English
team, that we had as much chance against the world champions as little Luxembourg would have had. We did not like
that, especially the Anglos. They had taken more of it than
we had. They had never heard the end of how England had
won the World Cup while we hadn't even qualified. Denis
Law, Jim Baxter and Billy Bremner were determined to win
and so was our newest Cap, Jim McCalliog of Sheffield Wed-
nesday. We all felt the same way and we didn't feel one little
bit afraid of the England team. We knew that we could beat
them. We had done it before, after all. In the Ramsey era we

had a better record against England than any other team in the world. Even now, he has had just one victory over us in seven years. It has not made him any more kindly disposed towards us. I have been told by English players that he always wants to beat us more than he wants to beat any other country...quite a compliment to a little country like Scotland!

That day was one of the finest days I've known in football. I captained a Scottish team that must have been as good as any in the past few years. Everyone know what they were expected to do and everyone achieved their objective. It was the first time, too, that Bobby Brown had been in charge of the full international team and as always, with a new boss, players tend to pull out that little bit extra. That happened at Wembley even though we had had to make a change at the very last minute. Little Jimmy Johnstone was injured in Celtic's European Cup semi-final against Dukla and had to call off on the Thursday morning. Willie Wallace flew down on Thursday night to take his place. The late change made no difference. Willie came in as if he'd been the first choice all along and we had England struggling right from the start.

I know that Jackie Charlton was injured and I know that a lot of English newspapermen used that as an excuse for the defeat. But, believe me, we would rather have had Charlton stay at centre-half. He was more of a problem to us when he came into attack than he had been in defence. Still, I always remember what Nobby Stiles said to me when the game was over. He made no excuses. He told me: 'You played much better today than any of us thought you could play. That's why you beat us. We didn't expect to find you playing as well as you did and some of us were not at our best. But Scotland deserved the win and we can't deny that.'

Nobby accepted it. We had been the better team. We had won. We had beaten the World Cup holders on Wembley, something that no other team in the world had been able to do.

For most of us, too, we had been able to prove that if we had had all our stars for our World Cup qualifying games we might have been able to qualify and give England a harder time than she had experienced.

Naples and our defeat from Italy rankled for a long time. We had been forced to go there without Law, without Baxter, without Billy Stevenson of Liverpool...all because English clubs wouldn't co-operate. That victory at Wembley helped to soften the harshness of the memory of Naples.

It also brought an honour to one of the greatest players in the game, and one of the nicest fellows, Ronnie Simpson of Celtic. If Ronnie's story had been written as a novel people would have laughed, it was so unbelievable. There he was at thirty-six years of age getting his first cap, getting it against England at Wembley when we won, and then going on to win a European Cup winners' medal. And the next season Ronnie stayed our first choice 'keeper. There was one simple reason for that . . . he was the best. I used to travel with him on the train from Edinburgh almost every morning and, believe me, few players deserve success more than Ronnie Simpson. All of us were delighted that he was in the team for his first cap that day, not just from sentiment, but also because he pulled off some of those remarkable saves of his when we might have landed in trouble.

When you watch Ronnie playing you wonder if he'll ever give up. He is as good now as he ever was. It wouldn't surprise me any if he's our goalkeeper in our World Cup bid in 1970.

We will be starting that bid next year some time, though the dates haven't been arranged. The draw has placed us in the same section as West Germany, Austria and Cyprus. Again we will probably run into problems when we need

Anglo-Scots for the games but we still feel that we can get to Mexico.

West Germany, beaten finalists at Wembley in 1966, are being marked down as the greatest danger and many people will be ready to write us off because we have to play them. I don't look at it that way. I have played against most of the players that West Germany will be using in their World Cup bid. With Rangers we've been drawn against a few German teams in the past couple of seasons and as I've said before I like facing the Germans. They play the game the way we do and that means a lot.

West Germany did reach the final of the World Cup but I saw something in that game that makes me feel we have a chance, a good chance ... the Germans were scared of England that day because they were playing them on Wembley. I think they will be the same when they come to Hampden to meet us. For instance, against England the West German boss made the same mistake as Bayern did against Rangers a year later, by playing Franz Beckenbauer as a defensive man. They played Beckenbauer against Bobby Charlton, marking Charlton in midfield, when, in fact, England would have been more concerned, more in danger, if Beckenbauer had been allowed to play the attacking game he had played in all the other World Cup games.

Their best players, for me, were the two men from Cologne, sweeper Wolfgang Weber and link man Wolfgang Overath. I played against both in a Fairs Cities' Cup game last year and my admiration for Overath increased enormously. He is a very talented, highly skilled player, a player who can become one of the world greats. He is far ahead of the highly praised German exile Helmut Haller who plays for the Italian side Bologna.

Overath will be one of the men that Schoen is building his team around. Weber will be another and so will the new

scoring sensation Johannes Lohr, another man who played for
Cologne. I know all three because I've played against them for
Rangers. I also know the goalkeeper Sepp Maier and Beckenbauer who both played for Bayern Munich and the Borussia
star Sigi Held. Most of these players will probably be used
against us and any Rangers' players in the Scotland team
will be able to assess them and help team boss Bobby Brown.

The Austrians aren't nearly so well known but already
Helmut Schoen has said that the Prater Stadium in Vienna
can be the graveyard of German and Scottish hopes. That
shows how much he thinks of the Austrian team and it shows,
too, that they could be as difficult a hurdle as the West
Germans. They have been re-building their team and have a
Vienna victory over Russia which is impressive. Their style is
like our own, they tackle hard and don't use the many dodges
on field that the Latin countries so often come up with.

The Cypriots are a different proposition. We know very
little about them, although we must look for a double victory,
home and away, over this tiny, unknown soccer country. The
heat, the food, the hard, bumpy condition that the pitch is
likely to be in, will all be against us. And also against us is
the fact that Scottish teams so often flop when they face the
easy-looking games....

We will have to watch that carefully this time. I know that
team manager Bobby Brown has plans to have a look at the
opposition as often as possible and that will help us tremendously. He will have a dossier on each country, a knowledge of their individual players and a run-down on their
tactics.

I feel that we have a great chance of reaching the finals
for the first time since 1958. Though obviously we could be
in trouble again if we cannot get our stars from England.

I hope that some arrangement can be worked out to help
us. Another Naples would break our hearts....

3

The stars—a personal assessment

ALTHOUGH I CRITICISED certain aspects of England's
World Cup win in the last chapter do not think that I have
only got bad things to say about the English team...I
haven't.

I admire most of the World Cup winners. As a fellow professional I was happy for them to win the World Cup. Yet
because of that, and because of my admiration for most of
them as players, I must still make plain the reservations I had
about that win. I've done that in the last chapter. Now in this
one I should like to give my own personal assessments of the
World Cup men. Assessments which, I would like to think,
carry some weight, coming from the captain of the first team
to defeat them, and the only team to be unbeaten against
them, since that World Cup victory.

To start with I'd like to say this—that there are two
players in this England team, Bobby Charlton and Geoff
Hurst, who I would rate in any world eleven I might be
asked to name. I don't make any apologies for looking at all-
star elevens in this way, players enjoy it as much as fans do.

These two would never be out of any team as far as I'm concerned and not far behind them I'd rate Nobby Stiles and
Alan Ball. They are two little players I have the highest regard
for. That they are not team certainties, like the other two, is
only because I feel they can be used for special games, in
specialist roles. The other two players rise above that kind of
classification; they are star material, players that cannot
be ignored.

The veteran left-back Ray Wilson would have been in-
cluded in my little list, too, a year or so back. But now, at
Ray's age, I think we have seen the best of him.

Anyhow, these are the principal stars to my mind, but here
I would like to give you my view of each of the eleven
players who helped win the World Cup, a view formed by
playing against them and, of course, formed when beating
them. . . .

Gordon Banks—There's no doubt in my mind that Gordon
is a first-class goalkeeper but he does have a weakness at cross
balls. There are times when he tries to get to a cross ball
that he loses the world class look he has at other times. As far
as direct shots are concerned he is tremendously agile for a
man of his size. Here he looks confident and classy. With
cross balls he can look almost amateurish. I think the understanding that he has with the other defenders—and they've
played together for a long time—helps him out when he gets
in trouble, helps him to recover from mistakes he makes with
crosses. But for my money Peter Bonetti of Chelsea is the
best goalkeeper England have.

George Cohen—I can never really understand how George
Cohen ever held his place in this World Cup team. As an
attacking full-back, an overlapping back—and he's supposed
to be one—he should achieve more. In modern football it has
become important to get behind a tight defence and a full-
back who overlaps can so often do this by getting into a posi-

tion behind the defence. I am afraid I have rarely seen Cohen do this. He takes the ball so far then sends a long high ball into goal . . . and many of these are wasted balls. What he does have is a burst of speed and most of the time he doesn't in my opinion even use that to its best advantage.

Ray Wilson—Ray is one of the world's best-ever full-backs. He is around thirty-three years old now and still stays as a top-class defender. He is very fast with a wonderful positional sense which is invaluable. It also helps England when their defences gets into trouble, because Wilson has the vital experience that can hold any defence together at a crisis point. His one weakness is that he is very left-footed and can struggle a little when a winger decides to cut inside him. I think, too, he likes to play against direct wingers rather than the tricky little men we have like Jimmy Johnstone or Willie Henderson. Yet, even if he is put in trouble by a winger I've never seen Wilson resort to dirty play. He remains a gentleman, one of the few players in the game today who would rarely deliberately foul another player.

Nobby Stiles—This little man from Manchester United had to wait a long time until he was finally recognised as a key man in the England team. There's nothing glamorous about Nobby. Very little polish or grace but, oh, how effective he is. He's never had a spectacular role with England or Manchester United and so it has taken longer than usual to recognise his special talents. In fact, it was not until the World Cup semi-final against Portugal that many fans finally accepted him. That was the night he went out to shadow Eusebio and managed to shackle him as no other player in the tournament had been able to do. Of course, even then it was a kind of second-hand recognition Nobby got, praise because Eusebio had become such a star. If he'd stopped a lesser player then he might still be struggling for recognition from

the fans. But Nobby was an essential part of that England
team. Without him, without his hard work, his tiger tackling
and his ability to read a game England wouldn't have done
so well. He is a ninety-minute man and a player who never
develops any big-time attitude. He will never be one of the
prima donnas. He will always be a man a manager can
depend on to do his job as well as he knows how.

Jack Charlton—Another man who remained under-rated
for too long . . . and another who was finally 'discovered' by
so many people only after the World Cup was won. He has
this tremendous height which, of course, makes him almost
unbeatable in the air. And with this ability he can cause a
load of trouble to opposing teams when he moves upfield for
corner kicks as we found out the year we beat England at
Wembley. Still, I always feel that an old-fashioned centre-
forward who takes the ball up to him can worry him and he
doesn't like being drawn out of the middle of the defence. If
he is drawn out then he loses the command he has in the
middle.

Bobby Moore—Always the first player to spot because of
that blond hair . . . and often under-estimated because of
the cool way that he does his job on the field. It is too easy to
write Bobby off as a glamour boy. He does a job of work and
he does it well. He lies back alongside Charlton as a second
centre-half and it's the easiest job on the field. I know because
I play it myself so often. And I think Bobby has made the
most of the position. He is not particularly fast but he conceals
this lack of pace with a knack for reading the game that few
other players possess. He is usually the last man in defence,
the back man and it is easy for him with his positional
ability to pick up the long balls that are hit past Charlton
and the other defenders. If there are any criticisms to be made
then I would say that sometimes when his team is in trouble
he is less inspiring than he should be. He seems content to stay

deep even when a game looks lost. He rarely comes out of that position in a bid to help push on attacks.

Alan Ball—A player who is out of the same mould as Nobby Stiles. But he has added to the fighting qualities of Nobby a brilliant individualism that anyone would want in their side. Even if he is having a bad game, a game where nothing is going right for him, he'll fight on. Alan Ball doesn't know what it means to give up, doesn't know what it means to hide as so many other players do when things run against them. He does a lot of damage with his running and his work rate is fantastic. No one I know gives more to his team and again, like Stiles, he is an essential part of this England team. He is the combative player they need, any team needs, if they are going to try to win the top honours in the game.

Roger Hunt—Roger is the type of front runner who never seems to tire, but he seems to lack the class of his World Cup partner, Geoff Hurst, or the man Ramsey preferred him to, Jimmy Greaves of Spurs. He is in because of his running power and his non-stop chasing for his team. On that basis it doesn't surprise me too much that Ramsey dropped Greaves in his favour. Jimmy Greaves very often did nothing in a team for eighty-five minutes then might suddenly snatch two brilliant goals. England wanted more than that. They wanted men who would run all day for the team, who would play for the full ninety minutes. They didn't want to carry a man on what he might do . . . they wanted a man who would do something all the time. Hunt was Ramsey's type of player. . . .

Bobby Charlton—In complete contrast to Hunt, Charlton is the graceful thoroughbred in the Ramsey stable. Charlton is the genius that Ramsey allowed in his team and Bobby is probably a greater player now, in the midfield, than he has been at any other time in his career. I remember him saying

once in a television interview that Manchester United's
assistant manager Jimmy Murphy had once told him that he
must never waste a ball . . . because it was so difficult in this
game to get possession of it. Once you did get possession the
rule was to make the ball do something for you. Charlton
has never forgotten that and it is stamped over his play . . .
because Bobby Charlton seldom wastes any ball. That lesson
he learned from Jimmy Murphy sums up his attitude to the
game as well as anything. Bobby, too, is the complete gentleman. I've never heard a player criticise Bobby or complain
about him. He is a player who rarely, if ever, retaliates when
he is fouled and who, of course, almost never commits a foul
himself. I've said that he uses a ball well. He also has a power
shot that few players can match and a body swerve that I've
never seen bettered. There is just one flaw in Bobby's make-
up . . . he never seems to become emotionally involved in any
game. He seems to glide through a game, almost above the
game, really. I would like to see him get angry, or annoyed
just once to see what effect it would have on his play. I think
that would add more bite, more spirit to his play. I feel that
a player can become greater if he allows himself to become
emotionally entangled in a game.

(I know that this works with me. And I've seen it work
with other players, too. With Dennis Law and Jim Baxter
and little Billy Bremner. I've seen these players become
niggled at something and then really begin to play. I wish,
just once, it would happen to Bobby—though not when I'm
playing against him. Because if it worked the way it does with
other players then his talent would become absolutely
frightening.)

Geoff Hurst—This is the second world-class man, the only
other player who stands up there alongside Bobby Charlton
all the time, in my book. He is the greatest goal getter in
Britain today, and probably in the world. He proves himself

week after week, season after season, by being up there leading the scoring lists in the English First Division while his
team, West Ham, struggle away down the League. His club
can have indifferent seasons yet Geoff Hurst goes right on
scoring goals and scoring goals is the most difficult job in
modern football. It is something that takes a special kind of
talent. A talent that can lift you high above ordinary team
performances and make you a great player in your own right.
Hurst is good in the air, and fast and dangerous anywhere in
the vital area around goal. He has a dangerous knack of
taking up vital and deadly scoring positions and he also has
the courage that is essential to any striker today. Hurst can
take the most punishing tackles and come back for more.
This marks him out, too, when courage is such a highly
thought of commodity in the competitive world of English
football.

Martin Peters—This is another player in the England team
that I cannot get excited about. Sir Alf has referred to him
as the greatest midfield player in the world...I can't see it.
He plays alongside one who is far and away his superior in
Bobby Charlton. I think that statement is just one that
many people cannot possibly agree with. I would never
rate him in the same class as Charlton, nor would I prefer
him to Stiles or Ball. He is in my opinion, a good
player, made to look better because he is in a good
team. If we are to judge his greatness, greatness in the terms
that Sir Alf has used, then, once again, we will have to wait
until Mexico in 1970. England are more likely to be up
against things there than they were at any time in the last
World Cup. For instance, think of the match where we beat
them at Wembley, where was Martin Peters that day? He
never once provided the impetus to his team that a player
of his supposed stature should have provided. Instead, he
did what I don't think a Ball or a Stiles will ever do, he hid.
—ACP

Even at Hampden when we drew 1–1 he was a better player in his own goalmouth than he was in midfield. I know he had a few shots at goal in that game, and, of course he scored, but that was because of people like Geoff Hurst who can create openings, who can make chances. Peters doesn't appear to make these kind of openings himself and surely creation must be the greatest attribute of a midfield player? I know that when we play England Martin Peters is usually the least of my worries. That is why I cannot look on him as an outstanding player. In a good team he can contribute something, in a struggling team he cannot, I feel, give the spur that a truly great player can provide. It may come but until it does then I'll just have to disagree with Sir Alf once again.

4

The Scot Symon era

TO MOST PEOPLE outside Ibrox Scot Symon, the man
who signed me for Rangers, the man who managed the club
for so long, was a distant and often difficult person.

He was, in fact, a bit of a mystery man to many, many
people. Most saw him as a quiet and reserved man. Yet
that was not the side of Scot Symon that we saw most often
inside the club. For once he started talking about football
he was a different man entirely. It was at these times the
really opened out. He would sit for hours talking about the
game, giving his views, listening to other people's arguments.
I did not always agree with him. I thought he was wrong in
certain things and I told him so but I respected him as a
manager because he knew the game inside out.

Once when we were travelling on one of these trips abroad
I told him that I wanted to become a football manager
when I finished playing—I still do, by the way. From then
on throughout the tour we used to have long discussions
about the game and about how a club should be managed.
He used to tell me how he would have played in certain

games and then he would listen to my views. We argued a lot because I saw things in different ways from him.

For instance, I used to say to him that when I became a manager I would never become a desk man. I believe in the track-suit manager. That's what I want to be myself one day, for it is the outdoor men who have been getting the results in the last few years.

Scot Symon could never by any stretch of the imagination be described as a track-suit boss. He used to point out that with a club such as Rangers there were many administrative duties for a manager to attend to. I used to say he should have other people to deal with that side of the business while he spent all the time with his players. That was not his way though. It had never been that way at Ibrox before he became manager and he didn't see any need to change the set-up. At that time I suppose he was following the tradition of Rangers' managers, a tradition that has only altered since he left.

But despite the fact that he rarely came out on to the training ground with us, and despite other disagreements I had with him, I respected him a lot. I understood his views on his job and I appreciated his deep knowledge of football.

He was often criticised, for example, because Rangers were said to be failures in Europe. In as far as we did not win a major European honour under his management then we were failures and so was he. But he was a 'failure', if we can call it such, in exactly the same way as Matt Busby of Manchester United, and Bill Shankly of Liverpool and Don Revie of Leeds and Harry Catterick of Everton, were 'failures'. Because none of these managers I've named, and they are among the best in Britain, have won a European trophy. That honour belongs to just three British club bosses, Bill Nicholson of Spurs whose team won the European Cup Winners' Cup, Jock Stein of Celtic who won the European

Cup, and Ron Greenwood of West Ham who won the European Cup Winners' Cup.

Yet, Scot Symon was often described as a failure in European football by the fans and the press. They ignored the fact that he twice led his team to the final of the European Cup Winners Cup and that he took them, too, to the semi-final of the European Cup.

All they remembered perhaps was the game when Real Madrid scored six goals against us in a European Cup first-round game in the Bernebeau Stadium. Or when Spurs knocked us out of the Cup Winners Cup. The successes he had were ignored ... simply because he didn't win one of the trophies.

The last time he took us to the final of the European Cup Winners' Cup—that was in his last full season—he had worked out defensive tactics which operated as well as any-one's defensive tactics!

In the games away from home he had us lying back in defence with Ronnie McKinnon and myself in the middle. He had the wingers placed wide on their wings ready to carry the ball, to hold it and to keep possession as long as possible. With our wingers, Willie Henderson and either Davy Wilson or Willie Johnston, at that time, the plans worked well in every round. It must have been very near a record to lose just five goals in nine matches in the second biggest of the European tournaments. That's what we did. We lost four goals away from home—including one in the final—and just one at home in all our games. Symon's tactics were largely responsible for that record and yet people still talk about him being a failure.

If he had had that record with any team other than Rangers he would no doubt have been lauded. But with Rangers it's different. You cannot be second best at any time. Even as players, we know that, for even after one bad game

the fans may start to boo. They want the best and they
won't be satisfied with anything less, even though it might be
only a fraction less.

I thought Scot Symon's tactics for these away games in
Europe were good. But I sometimes felt that he was not keen
enough to use modern developments. For instance, I used
to urge him to allow the full-backs to overlap much more
than they did in some games. Celtic were having success with
this method and so were other teams. I thought we would
have benefited by using the backs in this way too. But Scot
Symon did not see it my way. He always believed in the
wingers staying out on their wings. I remember Willie
Henderson getting into trouble with him often for wandering
inside and leaving his place on the touchline. The Boss
believed in a strict 4–2–4 formation with as few variations as
possible; it would be wrong to blame him for sticking to this
pattern when it had brought him so much success.

The thing that used to annoy me, though, was that Mr
Symon knew as much about the newer developments as anyone else at Ibrox. He just did not seem to want to use them.
One day at a special team talk he used a board with models
on it to illustrate tactics. When he was midway through his
talk I made a suggestion and he let me take the floor.

I thought that the team would benefit from a certain move
which had been used against us in a game the previous Saturday. While I was making my point, I was using the models
on the board to show exactly what I thought the team should
do in a certain situation. When I finished Mr Symon looked
at the board for a moment, moved some 'men' about himself
and said : 'If I was the opposing team that's how I would
stop you.'

The point was he had executed the move brilliantly. He
had made certain changes in the other team to counteract

the move I was suggesting. Before I could stop myself I blurted out: 'Why didn't you do that on Saturday then?'

There was a silence. I knew I was wrong but the words had come out before I realised what I was saying. The Boss didn't say anything. He just picked up that board, gathered the men together, put the whole lot under his arm and marched out of the room. We never saw the tactics' board again!

I don't know why he reacted like this: for that day he did exactly the right things. He showed just how we should have played when the opposition used this tactic against us the week before. He knew how to handle these new developments but I got the idea that it would have caused too much change, too much upset from the pattern he had always preferred.

Scot Symon, I suppose, was like the club in this way. He was conservative in his outlook, not too keen to change the way of football he had always stood by. Yet he could have changed to something new because he kept pace with the new ideas in football; he just didn't want to join in. He seemed to prefer the styles he had always known.

It was a shock to all the players at Ibrox when he left the club. It was probably a bigger shock to me than to any of the others, because the night before the announcement came that he had left Rangers after thirteen years as manager I had been with him in the BBC TV studios in Glasgow doing a tele-recording of the 'Quiz Ball' programme. We were up against Spurs and we lost, and after the show the Boss ran me to the station so that I could catch my train back to Edinburgh. All the time I was with him he never gave a hint of the storm that was going to break just twelve hours later. I've never seen him since that night.

The next morning we were told at training by Davie White, the present manager who was then Scot Symon's assistant, that Mr Symon had left the club. I think all of us were stunned. He had signed almost all the players who were present and I don't think any of us ever felt that he would leave. He seemed part of the club. For a while the lads kept finding themselves looking up towards the touchline at the Albion training ground as if expecting to see him there just as he used to be.

I must admit I learned a lot from him and I will always be grateful to him for that. We did not always agree but then I have strong views on the game and I like to state them. He had a different attitude, a different approach and because of this people, very often, did not get to know the depth of his football knowledge.

In all these long talks I had with him I never felt that he had been left behind by new ideas in football. Or by new tactics.

In fact, I remember on one trip to England, when we played Stoke City in a friendly, that he sat for hours discussing the game with top English managers, including Ron Greenwood of West Ham, who is rated one of the top football thinkers. Scot Symon held his own in that company... just as his tactics held their own in Europe in his last full season with the club.

I feel that Scot Symon just didn't want to change the tactics he had used for so long. He stuck by them because he believed in them, but not because he didn't know about modern trends.

And let us remember this—his ideas were good enough for Scottish football until the new Celtic emerged under Jock Stein. . . .

5
Into Europe

WHEN WE BEGAN our campaign in the European Cup
Winners' Cup two years ago we all realised that anything
less than victory in the tournament was going to be almost
total failure as far as our fans were concerned. This was
because right from the start of that season we were in the
shadow of Celtic. A few months before we had beaten them
in the Scottish Cup Final replay when our right-back Kai
Johansen scored with a great goal. That had been forgotten
by the time the season started.

Celtic, playing in the European Cup for the first time in
their history, were made firm favourites to win that cup by
the Glasgow bookmakers. A 4–1 pre-season victory over
Manchester United strengthened the hopes of their supporters and shortened the bookies' odds.

If we were to satisfy our fans then we had to do something
spectacular in the number two European tournament—the
European Cup Winners' Cup.

The club realised this too and before the season started
they spent almost £100,000 on two new players, inside-

right Alex Smith from Dunfermline and left-half Dave Smith
from Aberdeen. This was an unprecedented step by Rangers.
The highest fee they had ever paid before was £26,000 for
George McLean from St Mirren. The fees for the two Smith
boys dwarfed that.

But these buys made the fans realise that the club were
determined to keep up with Celtic and they stressed to the
players, too, that the challenge which Jock Stein had built at
Celtic Park had to be met.

Still, the public had to be convinced and despite the buys,
we were not rated as highly as Celtic in the European
competitions.

When the draw had been made a few weeks before the
start of the season we had been paired with the Irish club
Glentoran. We were happy enough with that. It looked the
kind of easy tie which would allow us to play ourselves into
Europe quietly, without too much difficulty. We were wrong.

As can so often happen in these games we looked for an
easy result when we travelled to Belfast. But it didn't turn out
that way. The Irishmen were bossed by player-manager John
Colrain, the ex-Celtic and Clyde centre-forward. Colrain had
been to watch us and had seen us lose disastrously to Celtic
in a Glasgow Cup game at Ibrox. He claimed he had seen
weaknesses. That was not taken seriously in Glasgow, or even
in Belfast because the Irish League team had been thrashed
12–0 by the English League the week before. A similar result
was expected. It did not materialise.

We attacked for most of the game and took the lead in
fifteen minutes when George McLean scored. After that we
did not play as well as we should have done.

Eventually, with literally the last kick of the game Glentoran levelled the scores at 1–1. Ironically, it was a goal
created by the only two Scots in their team—ex-Celt Colrain
pushed the ball to inside-right Billy Sinclair and the shot

from Sinclair went into the net from the post. That was our entry into Europe, our first step back after a season without European competition. It was a disaster for our supporters and around half the 40,000 crowd seemed to be our fans that night.

At the time we felt the same way as they did. We knew we should have won a game against a part-time team. Last season, though, we realised that the result had not been quite as bad as most folk thought. Glentoran went on to win the Irish League and, last season, they were in the European Cup, and were drawn against Benfica.

The famous 'Eagles of Lisbon', Eusebio and all, were twice held to a draw by the fighting Irishmen. The scores were 1–1 in Belfast and 0–0 in Lisbon. The rule which says that the team scoring most goals away from home took the proud Portuguese into the next round but there was little glory for them. They had found, just as we did, that you cannot under-estimate a team, especially a team whose manager has drilled his side into a very efficient outfit. The standard of their national game doesn't count all the time. It's what a team can be made to do on the big occasion that matters in Europe. We found that out before Benfica and we didn't like it.

When the Irishmen came to Ibrox we won 4–0. Our goals came from Willie Johnston, Dave Smith, Dennis Setterington and George McLean and this performance took us through to the second round with most of our self-respect restored.

Still, the doubts about our display in Ireland lingered and when the draw for the second round was made we found ourselves written off before a ball had been kicked. It did not please us any, but it was understandable. We had been drawn against the holders of the trophy, the tough Germans of Borussia Dortmund.

Dortmund was a side that no one needed to warn us

against. A few months before we were matched with them,
all Scotland had watched as they defeated Bill Shankly's
battle-hardened Liverpool side in the final of the Cup
Winners' Cup at Hampden. They had won 2–1 in extra
time against the men from Anfield, the men who had knocked
Celtic out in the semi-final.

I remembered that night at Hampden. The Germans had
been fit and tough, they had to be to defeat Liverpool! Since
that game we had seen some more of their stars play in
the World Cup finals in England. Three of them, goalkeeper,
Hans Tilkowski, centre-forward, Sigi Held, and outside-left,
Lothar Emmerich, had been in the West German team
beaten by England in the final of the Jules Rimet trophy.

The blond, speedy Held and the dark, burly, unpredict-
able Emmerich were rated the big danger men to us up
front. In the previous year's tournament Emmerich had
scored more goals than the entire Liverpool team.

We also knew that it would not be easy to get past their
giant centre-half Wolfgang Paul who had defied Liverpool's
attacking efforts at Hampden. Yet somehow I was not too
worried. I knew Dortmund were a good team but I felt we
could beat them. I suppose that is because I quite enjoy playing against the Germans. They play the game very much as
we do. They tackle hard and they do not resort to the jersey-
pulling tricks of some of the Latin players.

Despite that feeling of confidence, despite the fact that we
began to hit form near the ties, despite the fact that we
were a much better team than they were at Ibrox, we could
have lost the game because of a refereeing blunder. You learn
in European football to accept refereeing mistakes on matters
of interpretation. Some referees allow tackling to be as strong
as it normally is at home. Others do not and you learn to
adjust. This mistake, though, was not in that category. It was
a major error which was condemned by almost every top

Scottish referee when a newspaper conducted an after-the-match poll on the incident.

It happened this way.... We had taken the lead in ten minutes when Kai Johansen—he makes a habit of getting these vital goals—scored. He gave us the start we had been looking for and the 65,000 fans were behind us all the way. Then came the mistake by the Spanish referee Daniel Zariquiegui. Sigi Held had taken the ball down the left wing in one of his long runs. He crossed the ball and ran over the by-line after he had done so. The ball went right across to the other side of our penalty box where the German full-back Peehs picked it up. As he gathered it ready to send it back into our goal Held stayed off the field of play, knowing that he could be given off-side if he came back. Then Peehs crossed the ball and I tried to clear it. It struck my leg and broke away across our goal again. As that happened Held made up his mind to come back on to the field, got to the ball as we stood appealing and slipped it to his inside-right Trimhold who scored. We didn't think it possible that the referee would allow the goal. We protested when he turned to run to the centre circle. We couldn't believe it possible that he would allow the goal to stand. Yet the Spanish referee did.

What happened, in fact, was that he gave Held a double benefit. He allowed him to remain off the field of play when the ball was crossed, so avoiding moving into an off-side position. Then, when the ball struck me, he allowed him to return and did not give off-side against him because the ball had struck a defender. Held had deliberately stayed off the field and as soon as he came back the game should have been stopped. Anyhow, it was not and we went to Dortmund with just a one goal lead, gained when Alex Smith scored with a second-half header.

Our chances looked slim, desperately slim. No British team

had beaten Borussia in a European tournament for two years and no one gave us the slightest hope of holding them on their own Rote Erde Stadium.

When we lost to Dunfermline in a league game the day before we flew out the chances appeared even less. That result did not help our confidence and we knew that under the rules of the Cup Winners' Cup tournament Borussia had just to score one goal to reach the next round. Their goal at Ibrox would count double if the scores were level on aggregate.

Dortmund were sure they could do it. Held and Emmerich had stated it publicly ever since they returned from the Glasgow game. West Ham—Bobby Moore and all—had gone to their Rote Erde Stadium less than a year before and been beaten. They could not see Rangers stopping them getting the one goal they needed to hold on to their trophy.

And yet, it was Lothar Emmerich, the Germans' goal scoring star, who did as much as anyone to make sure that we did hold out. He did it when he fouled our inside-right Bobby Watson in the thirty-eighth minute. Watson had been one of our key men as we set up a defensive barrier against the Germans. Then after a corner kick the ball was cleared and Bobby was left lying in a heap on the edge of our box after a tackle by Emmerich. It appeared to be a foul and Bobby was carried off on a stretcher. We were furious. We had been playing well before this, and defending stubbornly. But that injury to Bobby Watson strengthened our determination to reach the next round. We were determined to get there for his sake and also to show Emmerich that his type of tackle would not help his team.

Bobby was able to come out on to the trainer's bench in the second half and sat there encouraging us. It has happened before that an injury blow like the one we faced that night can inspire a team and it certainly inspired us that night in Dortmund.

The hundreds of fans who were there to cheer us—not all of them thought we had no chance—saw Alex Smith drop back to take Bobby Watson's role and saw the defence hang on until the end. The score stayed at 0–0 and we were through. In fact, we had the best chance of the game when centre-forward Jim Forrest, now with Preston, shot past when a Willie Johnston pass put him through. That's how close we were to a victory that night.

But victory in that one game was not important. All that mattered was that we reached the next round of the competition and a 0–0 draw was enough to take us there.

That's how things go in European football, of course. The results of individual games don't settle things; it is the results you get over the two games that matter. To get a victory away from home is a great achievement but it's just about as commendable to get a draw. We went to Dortmund knowing that a draw was good enough to take us through to the third round. And so it was.

The way we played wouldn't make us many friends among the Borussia supporters in the stadium that night. The 40,000 who were there must have been completely frustrated watching us pull everything back into defence, just as our supporters get fed up when a team throws up a similar defensive curtain at Ibrox.

But there was no alternative for us. We could not afford to lose one goal. One goal would have meant defeat, one goal would have meant that our supporters had been let down again. We did not want that so we drew into a defensive shell which gave us the result we wanted.

This is an integral part of European football. I know that Celtic's victory over Inter-Milan in Lisbon was hailed as a victory for attacking football. Yet from my own experiences last season it still has not had any lasting effect on European football. And remember that was one match, with no home and away ties. In the semi-finals against Dukla when Celtic knew that the greatest prize in club football was within their grasp they went to Prague and put up the shutters.

The rule that now says that away goals will count double in the event of a draw on aggregate scores has helped a little.

Teams realise now that they must try to snatch a goal on the break out of defence. But their tactics away from home are still based mainly on a tight defensive structure. It cannot be any other way unless the opposition is weak.

At the top level, though, the pattern will not change. It will stay as uncompromising defence when you are away from home and all-out attack, looking for the goals that count, when you are backed by your own fans at your own ground.

Gordon Banks is beaten for Scotland's only goal at Hampden in the 1-1 draw last season

The Scottish Cup Final at Hampden between Rangers and Celtic two years ago. Skipper John Greig runs in as 'keeper Billy Ritchie watches the ball sneak past

The goal that ended Rangers' hopes at Elland Road in the
Fairs Cup semi-final against Leeds United. Giles' penalty flies
wide of 'keeper Sorensen

Greig heads clear in the first game against Leeds as Peter Lorimer
challenges

Nuremberg . . . and the disallowed goal from Roger Hynd that
Greig felt might have changed that European Cup Winners Cup
Final against Bayern Munich

Goalkeeper Norrie Martin saves from Bayern's Gerd Muller,
on the ground after being tackled by Kai Johansen while Greig
stands by

Greig is there in his cover role as Dave Provan heads clear in a Bayern attack in the European Cup Winners Cup final in Nuremberg

Greig is swamped by his team mates after he had scored the vital goal against Italy in the World Cup

6

The road to the Final

THAT GAME in Dortmund was our toughest in Europe
that season...but the one against the Spanish team Real
Saragossa did not come far behind it. And, in the final sum-
ming-up, I rated the Spaniards as the finest team we met that
year.

Earlier in the tournament they had been able to defeat
Everton, the English Cup winners. We knew how much that
result meant. Everton had big money men in their team.
They had international stars scattered through their side and,
of course, the standard of English football is so often rated
much higher than our standard in Scotland. Mind you, this
is something I don't always agree with.

Still, we knew that the game was going to be hard and we
knew, too, that we were facing a fine footballing team. Alex
Smith had played against the Spaniards for Dunfermline
the previous season in the Fairs Cities' Cup tournament and
he gave us the low-down. Their forward line was rated as
the greatest club forward line in Europe. At outside-right
they had the veteran Canario, a man who had been in the

fabulous Real Madrid front rank when they defeated Eintrach Frankfurt in that European Cup Final at Hampden....

At centre-forward they had the powerful Marcelino, a bustling goal scoring idol in Spain.... At outside-left they had the graceful Lapetra who was a regular in the Spanish national team. At inside-forward they had Santos, the man I thought was their best player and Villa, another vital player in the forward-line—known as the Magnificent Five.

Flurries of snow and sleet bit into our faces when we took the field for the first match at Ibrox. The conditions were in our favour but, even allowing for that, we put on an impressive display for the 65,000 fans who were there to see the game.

We played open attractive football and Dave Smith had the finest game he had had since joining Rangers from Aberdeen. It was his night more than anyone else's and he scored the opening goal in ten minutes when our other big money buy Alex Smith put him through. Alex Willoughby scored a second before half-time and each of the scorers had goals disallowed for off-side. The Spaniards managed just one chance in the entire game when Canario had an opening four minutes from the end but missed it.

It might have been a better score for us but we were happy with a two-goal lead. We were beginning to feel now that this could be our year to win a major European honour. After all, we had knocked out the holders Borussia Dortmund and now we were poised to beat the favourites, Saragossa.

We had not had a two-goal lead to take to Dortmund and we got through; we couldn't see that we would do worse in Spain.

These were the thoughts in our minds as we prepared for the visit to Spain but none of us realised the drama that was to hit us in the Romareda Stadium. I am glad we didn't because it gave me one of my worst moments in football, a moment I'll never forget.

However, that comes a little bit later in the story of the game. The trouble for us in this match began before we left Glasgow. We were playing a league game at Ayr on the Saturday, two days before we flew to Saragossa. It seemed the ideal fixture to have before going off into Europe. Ayr had not won a game in the First Division and we did not expect too much trouble. We did not get it. We won easily but towards the end of the game centre-half Ronnie McKinnon collided with one of the Ayr forwards and reeled away holding his nose. That was it.

Ronnie's nose was found to be broken and manager Scot Symon named young Colin Jackson as his replacement for the European match. Colin had played for the first team a few weeks before this in a friendly game at left-half. This was his first real taste of big-time soccer and he couldn't have picked a harder match.

But the manager was right in naming him immediately; it let everyone know what the team was going to be. There was no dressing-room speculation, and there was no major team shuffle where one or more positions might conceivably have been weakened. It was a straight swop—Colin Jackson for the injured Ronnie McKinnon. The Spaniards had changed their team, too. Canario was dropped and a new young star Bustillo was brought in.

Colin Jackson played well. I stayed close to him at the start, closer than I would have if Ronnie had been there. But he settled quickly and he held Marcelino magnificently.

We did not lose a goal until well into the second half when Lapetra scored from a free kick. Still, it looked as if that was the only one the Spaniards would get and we had an Alex Willoughby goal disallowed for off-side.

Then with two minutes left to time and as Saragossa

thundered against our defence with tremendous pressure, the French referee, Michel Kitabjian, gave a penalty against us. The ball was sent into our box and I breasted it down before clearing. The referee claimed I had handled. I had not and I still say so today. He was mistaken. But the mistake allowed Villa to net from the spot and carry the game into extra time.

And tragedy again for us here when Dave Smith missed a penalty for us in the fourth minute of extra time. We dominated that extra half hour but we couldn't score and we were still locked together at the end of it.

And that's what brought me the moment I never want to face again. It made me one of the central figures in those farcical toss-of-the-coin dramas which football uses to separate two teams who have not been able to reach a result on the field.

What made it worse for me was that I had won the toss twice already, at the start of the game and again when we moved into that extra half hour. I couldn't see that the luck would hold out for this third time, this most crucial time of all.

I spoke to the manager and between us we decided to call tails. On the coin, a French two-franc piece, the tail was a figure 2.

I stood out there on the field along with the referee and the Spanish skipper, the left-back Reija. The coin spun into the air and was carried away from our little group by the wind. The referee reached it first and covered it, then when we were together he let us look at the coin and there it was with that silver two gleaming up at me. I literally jumped with joy and so did the manager. Willie Henderson turned cartwheels round the field and trainer Davie Kinnear went to the dressing-rooms to tell the boys who could not bear to stay and watch the toss. It was a deliriously happy moment for us although I felt sympathy for little Reija as he walked in tears to his dressing-room. I would have been the same if I had lost that toss.

Let me say now that I think this method is the wrong way to settle an important match. If I had lost people would have thought it was sour grapes if I had spoken my mind. But I am talking now after winning, after being put through to the European Cup Winners' Cup semi-final by the toss of a coin. And I say it is ridiculous. Yet it is the rule governing the major European tournaments. It is the rule which governs even the World Cup but I cannot agree with it and I do not think any professional footballer does. I do not see how anyone can agree that a gamble should settle a game where so much effort has been expended in a bid for victory.

I don't know what the best alternative would be, though, in the Cup Winners' Cup I think that a third game on a neutral ground should be tried before they reach this last resort.

If that idea does not work then the teams should perhaps take penalty kicks until a decision is arrived at that way. I don't think counting corners is the answer when teams often try to defend in these matches. Penalties would be a better idea. It is not ideal but it is a whole lot better than seeing your football future being spun high in the air by a referee.

I have the coin used that day in my house now as a souvenir. On the night of the game I had not had a chance to try to get it from the referee. But Davie Kinnear did. He went to the referee's room and talked him into parting with the coin. The next day on the flight home he presented it to me.

Winning the toss caused a stir among the fans and it continued on the Saturday at Ibrox when we met Hibs. I went up to toss the coin at the start of the game and there was almost a hush as the fans waited to see if I could win again.

Amazingly enough I did and the fans roared out their pleasure.

We had known the draw for the Cup Winners' Cup semifinals before we played the match in Saragossa. We had been drawn against the team we considered the easiest opposition left, Slavia Sofia of Bulgaria. The other match was between the Germans, Bayern Munich, and the Belgians, Standard Liege.

The Bulgarians were unknown to us. No Scottish team had ever played there before. All we knew about Bulgarian football was the little we had seen of their international team during the World Cup in England when they had been in the same section as Portugal, Hungary and Brazil.

The joy we felt about drawing Slavia continued until we saw the ground where we were to play the game. Up to that time everything had been perfect. The food was much better than we had hoped for. When we trained at Slavia's own stadium the condition of the pitch was ideal and the training ground they allowed us to use was perfect for our requirements.

When we were told that the match would be played on the national stadium, the Levski Stadium, we felt even happier. We expected some kind of Eastern European Wembley. We didn't get it.

We were impressed as we drove up. The stadium was set among trees and overlooked by a mountain, its top lost in the mists. It was a sight to be remembered. But the pitch was a different story. There was scarcely any grass on it and what little there was, was growing in rough clumps which would make ball control very difficult. The centre circle was completely bare and so were the two goalmouths.

To make things even worse repairs were being made at the ground and right round the edge of the playing field there were iron pipes and metal spikes which were dangerously close to the touchline. As Willie Henderson put it: 'There are better pitches on Glasgow Green...'

Yet this was the venue for the European Cup Winners' Cup semi-final. In most countries it would have been laughable but behind the Iron Curtain anything can happen and all you can do is accept it. We knew we had to play and we knew that moans and complaints would not help us any.

We could have protested but after all, we were going into these countries as ambassadors. That kind of protest might have been construed as bad sportsmanship so we took it quietly and went back to our hotel.

In the end our worries proved unnecessary because Slavia were the poorest team we had met in the tournament. They were tough and reasonably skilful but they never had us in any trouble. Davy Wilson scored a goal to give us victory on their ramshackle pitch and we knew then that we had probably done enough to reach the tournament final for the second time.

We still had to face the game at Ibrox but we had gained a victory away from home. In front of our own fans we were sure that we wouldn't fail.

The manager made team changes for that game. Roger Hynd came in at centre-forward. It was a shock choice though he had been playing in the reserves as centre. I think even big Roger was shattered when the Boss announced that he would be playing. He came in and he tried as hard as he knew how and again the team won. Again the score was 1–0 and this time it was a goal from Willie Henderson which brought us the result.

We knew, too, that we would meet Bayern Munich in the final and their coach, the burly little Yugoslav Zlatko Cajkowski, watched us against the Bulgarians in that second match.

We had made the final. We had been able to hang on to

Celtic just as we had wanted to do from the start of that season. Always their successes, or expected successes, in the European Cup had acted as an extra spur to us in our own tournament.

We knew that we were in the secondary tournament, that Celtic were in the big one. But, still we were there in the final, just as Celtic were in the final of the European Cup.

It was an amazing double for Glasgow, a fantastic double that no European city has ever had, a team in each of the two major European finals!

Celtic were in one final and we were in the other and our fans stayed happy. We hadn't let them down. Their Parkhead rivals could say that they were in the top tournament and we were second to them but we were in the final just the same as their team.

The one difference was that our final was to be played in Germany, the country where our opponents came from. It was scheduled for Nuremberg as it had been for months and that meant that the Bayern team would be enjoying a home game.

Nuremberg was just over a hundred miles from Munich. The Bayern fans would flood down the autobahns and our support would be hopelessly outnumbered.

We realised that this was going to be very hard....

7

The big disappointment

LOOKING BACK at these two games, the two finals that
meant so much to Glasgow and to the whole of Scotland, the
games in Lisbon and Nuremberg, I wish we had been able
to play our game first.

The pressure that hit us as we prepared for the game
against the Germans became even greater when Celtic won,
and won well, in Lisbon. Everyone in European football had
watched their game and seen their style of play. They had
hailed them as the new leaders, the first team to go all out
in attack in European football since Inter began to dominate
the Continent a few years beforehand. Less than a week
later we were going to be compared with them. And we also
had to win to make the second half of the double reality.

I never felt at any time that season that there was a big
gap between ourselves and Celtic. I wasn't scared of playing
against them. And on the display in our closing game at
Ibrox against them when we drew 2–2 I thought we had
proved ourselves. But comparing the styles of play was something else.

We had marched through Europe—and through the Scottish League competition, too—with tactics that were based on strong defence. We had not scored too many goals. Our successes had come through preventing the other teams from scoring.

In fact, all the way through the year our scoring record had been so bad, and the form of our strikers so unconvincing, that we had always worried about losing the first goal. A lot of the boys in the team had the feeling that if we ever went behind in a match then we would never be able to get the goal back....

In Europe this had never happened. In all our ties we had gone in front first and the fear we had with us had not been tested.

Still, the views of the European journalists and football officials was another burden we carried with us to Nuremberg. They wanted our game to be like the Lisbon game, fast, open, attractive, and we knew that our opponents played in a similar style to us. They were a cautious team, and if anything we felt that they were a little bit frightened of us. We had that impression before the game and it stayed with us when we eventually played them. In these circumstances it was difficult to anticipate a classic game such as the one in Lisbon had been. We all knew that when we flew into Germany.

Our manager, Scot Symon, had watched Bayern play in a German league game against Kaiserslautern. He had told us of the style they played, examined the tactics and pinpointed the danger men. He warned us that Franz Beckenbauer, the midfield genius of the West German World Cup team was shackled to a sweeper's role, playing behind the rest of the Bayern defence.

That was a shock to most of us because we had expected that Beckenbauer in his normal role would have been the main danger to us. We expected to have to hold him in mid-field, stop him getting into dangerous attacking positions, and now we were told that he did not attack!

After that trip the Boss made we had several warm-up games, in Toronto against the Czech champions Sparta Prague, against Morton and against Motherwell. The games in Scotland were just to keep us in trim, help us stay match fit, so to speak. The Motherwell game was a benefit for Charlie Aitken and their team was reinforced by players like Dave Mackay of Spurs and Ian St John and Billy Stevenson of Liverpool. That tested us a bit but not as much as the game in Canada.

We had thought that this would keep us thinking in terms of European football; we didn't realise how right that was. The game was meant to be a show game to help build up soccer in the United States and Canada but the Czechs turned it into a European Cup tie. Our fans had come to Toronto from all over Canada, waving their colours, singing their songs as if they had never left home. It was a gala occasion for these exiles but for Sparta it was a chance of building their soccer prestige. Nothing else was in their minds.

Sparta scored a goal against us early on before we had even settled and then immediately dropped back into defence. They defended as toughly and as roughly as if we were playing in the Cup Winners' Cup Final a few weeks early. We found ourselves being tackled hard and viciously by a team who were out to make a name for themselves. In the end they held on to win because we could not find a way round their packed defence and they went home to Prague happy. They were the only happy people. Our fans were disappointed. We were disappointed because we had let them down and the sponsors who had wanted the game as a boost to football there were unhappiest of all.

Just over two weeks later we were flying into Nuremberg

Airport for a three days stay in which nothing went right. For a start it had been decided that we would make our training headquarters out in the country at a tiny village called Neundettelsau. The idea was that if we were staying out there in a secluded hotel we would be clear of the fans, clear of people looking for tickets, clear of autograph hunters and able to sleep at night without worrying about a city's traffic. It sounded fine in theory but it proved to be a mistake. We were twenty miles out of the city and the training facilities we had were terrible. On our first afternoon there we went down to the little local training ground to have a loosening up session and found the gates locked. We had to hang around for half an hour until someone came to open them up and let us in. The journeys in and out of the city weren't any help either.

Twenty miles doesn't sound very far but this journey was along narrow twisting country roads and the bus journey took an hour. Few of the lads like being cooped up in a bus like that.

Then, the idea of getting us away from the tension and the build-up to the game backfired. The hotel was so lacking in atmosphere that I am convinced that we lost our edge a little. We scarcely knew there was a game on. No buzz, no noise from outside, no feeling around that something big was going on. The place was like a morgue so we sat around playing cards or talking about the game. There was so little to do that the boys became bored and the bus trips in between cnly made things worse.

The game, too, went badly. Franz Roth had been named by the manager as the danger man and, ironically, he was the one who got the extra time goal which defeated us. That was just one more of the Nuremberg mistakes, a mistake made by a single player who admitted that he should have been with Roth when he burst through to score. He blamed

himself in the dressing-room after the game but we could
not allow him to take all the blame. This was a night when
the team failed right through the match. We all had responsi-
bilities. I realise now that our tactics were wrong and they
should have been changed during the game.

They had seemed OK when we were having our team talk
before the game. The idea was that we could win the game
down the wings using Willie Henderson and Willie Johnston
who was back in the team after recovering from an ankle
break. The snag here was that the German full-backs lay
out very wide on the two wingers. They marked them tight,
as tight as I've ever seen any two players marked. And if
they tried to wander the backs went with them. We were in
trouble from then on. We should have varied our play when
we saw what was happening. We didn't. We should have
tried dropping balls behind the full-backs so that our wing
men could run on to them. We didn't do that enough, either.

And, even if we had done that, these balls would probably
have been swallowed up by the immaculate Beckenbauer.
He had the undemanding job of sweeper and he did it per-
fectly. Never once did he make a mistake. Never once did we
get him ruffled, though we had hoped that the power of
Roger Hynd in the middle would upset him. And only once
did he come upfield in the one hundred and twenty minutes
it took to separate us.

I admired Beckenbauer for the way he did that job that
night, the job he was being asked to do by his club team.
Yet to me it was a waste of talent. There are few men in the
world who have his genius for attacking from midfield positions. The German team boss Helmut Schoen still plays him
there in the national team and he'll be a tremendous danger
to Scotland when we face them in the World Cup qualifying
games.

That is when we will be up against him in the role where

he can do most damage with his unique talents. Yet Bayern sacrificed these talents for safety. They were not as good a team as Borussia had been, not as good as Saragossa either, and yet they willingly threw away the greatest midfield man in Europe so that they could play safety-first soccer. It was a strange decision because they had few men of real talent in the side.

I liked their goalkeeper Sepp Maier who has now become keeper for the national team. I liked the deep lying inside-forward Dieter Koulmann who was clever and good on the ball and I liked the other midfield man, the powerful Franz Roth, the man who took the trophy we wanted so much from us.

We had created as many scoring chances as them. We had been ahead of them in everything but goals . . . and we had had a goal disallowed just as we had had in Saragossa. Then in the nineteenth minute of extra time came the goal which swept away our dreams and destroyed the chance of the European double we had fought so hard for. It also left us in the position of not having won a single trophy that season. . . .

To Roth and to Bayern that goal meant winning the European Cup Winners' Cup and all the glory that goes with it.

To us the goal meant more than simply losing that trophy . . . it meant disaster. It meant that we had failed our fans again, by not keeping up with Celtic in Europe after failing against them at home. They had won everything they had played for . . . we had won nothing.

For the first time in my life I was crying as I walked off that field. All the disappointments of the season came back and hit me as the German players were surrounded by their cheering fans and we were left to come off beaten and dejected. I wept then and I couldn't help myself. It had all been too much. We had been so close to doing something that no Rangers' team before us had done and we had seen it snatched away. It was almost as if these great teams of the past were mocking us. . . .

All of us felt the same. Roger Hynd was so bad that he hurled his runners'-up medal into the crowd after the presentation. He didn't even look at it, just tossed it away into that sea of faces around us. It was only later that he found out that the medals we received were the same as winners' medals. It was too late then, though and Roger hasn't seen that medal since Nuremberg. It's probably a souvenir in some German home right now.

The journey back to that little hotel in the country after the banquet was like a funeral procession. When we got there the Boss left us in the hall, went straight to his room and locked the door. We didn't see him again until we were leaving the following day. I've never known him take a result so badly.

The really sickening thought that hit us all when we were sitting there in that hotel thinking back on the game was that they had been frightened of us. They were more worried about us than we had been about playing them. They had had the backing of that huge crowd. It was a home game for them and the real responsibility of attacking should have lain with them. They didn't take it up. They threw away that initiative because they were afraid of us.

That was why they had made such a fuss of getting their centre-forward Gerd Muller fit to play against us. Muller had broken his arm in an international against Yugoslavia a month or so before we played them. He made his comeback for Bayern just four days before they met us, wearing a heavy leather covering on the arm for support. They wanted special permission from the Italian referee Concetto Lo Bello to allow him to play with the strapping on the damaged arm. They didn't get it. He had to alter the strapping considerably before he was allowed to play. When he did it was obvious to all of us that he wasn't match fit. He was carrying extra weight and he made no impression on the game at all. Yet they had been desperate to get him in the team. That proved to me that even with the advantage of playing in their own country they had not been confident of beating us. If we had been in a neutral country things might have been different.

Still, they beat us and that's that. The details I've given you aren't meant to be excuses. They are reasons why we lost the game. We don't need excuses ... we accepted the blame for defeat as a team.

Before finishing the Nuremberg story I would like to say one more thing. The day before the game the club chairman Mr John Lawrence held a press conference and was heavily criticised by the Scottish newspapers for remarks he made at it about the team. It has been suggested that these remarks and the heavy press coverage of the affair affected our play. It didn't.

We didn't even know about the conference until after the game when someone gave us the papers from home. It had happened in Nuremberg and in our secluded little hotel we had heard nothing at all about it. It had no effect on our performance that night.

The team were out on the field and the team accepted the blame.

8

New man at Ibrox

I FEEL CERTAIN that a soccer revolution will be taking place inside Ranger's Football Club to bring back the honours we have missed over the past two seasons. A revolution that was delayed only by Davie White because he knew very well that he could not introduce all his own ideas within a few weeks of taking over as manager, and he could not change the set-up while the team was leading the Scottish First Division and in the running for all the major honours.

Many people would imagine that taking over a team at the top of the league, a team challenging for the Fairs Cities' Cup and favourites along with Celtic for the Scottish Cup was an easy thing. I don't. The way I see it is that all these things made the job of being manager of Rangers a very difficult one when Davie White was appointed to take over the team after Scot Symon had left the club.

For a start, the new Boss had his own personal ideas on the game, firm and strong ideas on tactics and training. At Clyde. where he had been manager for a full season, taking over more or less at the start of a new season, he had been able to express these ideas more easily because pressure on the club was not nearly so great. So his ideas went into practice and Clyde, a part-time team, finished third in the First Division behind Celtic and ourselves.

At Ibrox it was all so different. Here the Boss was faced with the job of taking over a team already at the top, a team he could take no higher in the league.

And here, even though some of the ideas on training and on the side's approach to the game weren't exactly what he wanted, he couldn't make drastic alterations. He knew that to change things radically at that stage of the season was to look for trouble. To change then wasn't really feasible if the team's run of success was to continue. And, of course, it continued until almost the end of the season.

He was able to make modifications. He was able to make slight changes in our schedules, but no more. The biggest change, of course, was that he came out to the Albion training ground and worked out with us. He is a young manager, a track-suit manager, a manager who trains with his players and that was something we hadn't known before. The previous manager, Scot Symon, had been a follower of the Bill Struth tradition at Ibrox, the tradition that kept the manager that bit aloof from his players. This was something very different and it was something that every player welcomed.

For example, when we were out on the training ground we would may be try to work out a variety of moves to be used in games but manager Scot Symon was very often not there to see them. This has altered tremendously. Now we have the manager with us all the time, going over the previous games and the mistakes that we made in them, working out new moves, suggesting fresh ideas for dead ball moves at corners and free kicks. He brought ideas with him and these ideas were used without upsetting the routine, the system we had been accustomed to.

We used some of these ideas in our games for, after all, these are the things that football thrives upon. You cannot stand still in football. You must always be ready to listen and learn from other people, to try out new ideas of your own. Without this sort of approach the game would begin to die. The game is developing all the time and every club and every player must be ready to go with it. If you don't then you are left behind and that is committing soccer suicide.

Davie White is the type of manager who believes in moving forward all the time, in advancing with the game, keeping step with the new ideas. He always tries to see the games that matter in European football, the games where a lot can be learned from studying the teams in action.

He showed that side of himself when he was with Clyde. Remember, he was the only Scottish manager who travelled to see Celtic play Inter-Milan in Lisbon in the European Cup Final and then went on to Nuremberg to watch us play Bayern Munich in the European Cup Winners' Cup Final. He had the chance the next season of leading Clyde into Europe—a chance that eventually never arrived—and he wanted to learn from the two top European show games. He was eager to study, ambitious to see the best teams in Europe play, ambitious to learn enough to have a crack at the top level in these competitions himself. As a player with Clyde he did not have the chance to play in Continental tournaments. He is first to admit that some of the Rangers' players have more experience at this level than he does. But he sees everything that he can, he picks up as much as he can, and that shows he is heading in the right direction.

It was not Davie White's fault that we lost against Leeds. There were happenings in these games that were beyond the control of the manager, of any manager in fact. It was the same when we eventually lost the league title. We made the mistakes out on the field. There were occasions when we just

didn't do what we had been told to do by the Boss. It wasn't
that we had deliberately disobeyed his pre-match instructions,
it was simply that we allowed the games to run out of our
control and then weren't able to settle to the things the Boss
had outlined beforehand.

There were some changes he made in our general playing
pattern. He asked our two wingers to play deeper than they
had ever done before. In the past Rangers had their wingers
playing well upfield, out on their touchlines, often ending up
marking the full-back instead of getting away from him!
Now they have been told to drop back, moving clear of the
opposition full-back, hoping they can collect the ball un-
marked and then be able to run with it and start a move.
There was another reason for this change too. Often nowa-
days you find yourself coming up against a 4–3–3 set-up. If
you are playing 4–2–4—our normal formation—you can find
that you will be caught out by the extra man the opposition
have in the middle of the park. If the wingers come deep then
you can counter-act this by having, for spells, what is almost
a 4–4–2 set-up. It balances the position in the middle, swing-
ing it, in fact, in your favour, and it provides the wingers
with more opportunities to set up attacking moves.

In the training, too, there were little differences. The new
manager introduced more competition into the training
sessions. He had us playing many more practice games than
we had ever done. He had us competing against each other
in various different ways. He had the strikers working at their
shooting from through balls and from cut-backs coming at
them from the by-lines.

It was all much more urgent than we had known it before.
And the extra practice games—we played a side every day—
helped to build team understanding. Before the change we
had sometimes just one single practice game a week, with
maybe two in special circumstances. We didn't have the

specialised group training that we were given last season. And these changes are only a beginning.

The Boss has spoken to me as skipper and told me of some of his plans. I know that these tiny—but important—modifications were all that he could do in his first seven months as manager but now he has more opportunity to make further changes. More chance to express his own ideas as he wants to express them.

These changes will be introduced on the field, at training sessions and off the field, too, probably. Although he himself is a break with tradition, someone who came from outside the club as well as a track-suit manager who mixes with his players, he still respects that tradition that has been built up at Ibrox. He already insists that we travel to all our games wearing the club blazer and flannels. He will probably have more ideas on these lines.

On the field, too, I know that he wants to change some aspects of our play. I don't think that we will be playing the same kind of game much longer. I think that when the Boss's ideas really start to be expressed inside the club we will be playing better football, smoother football than we have ever done before. If there had been time in his first season it would have happened but there was no opportunity to work on major changes. He was given a team at the top and to change a winning team, a successful team, was too big a gamble for anyone to take. After all, can a team really be asked to alter their style of play midway through a season. No manager would ever ask that. If you were taking over a team at the bottom of the table, however, things would be different. You can afford to try out ideas then; you can afford to ask for major changes in tactics because the only way you can go is up.

But once you start tampering with a successful formula and our formula was successful—it had taken us to the final of the

European Cup Winners' Cup and it had placed us on top of the league—then you can land the team in trouble. It was not a risk for a manager to take at that time. That's what I meant when I said it was harder for the Boss to take over the team when it was at the top than it had been for him to take over little, part-time Clyde.

When he took over there had been few problems with the players. I have heard a lot about ex-players taking over as managers teams which contain players they have played with or against and finding the situation difficult. This didn't happen at Ibrox even though most of the lads had played against the Boss when he was Clyde's skipper.

What possibly helped to ease any problems that might have cropped up was the fact that the Boss spent a few months as assistant manager when he first came from Clyde. In that way we had all become used to him in a position of authority at the ground. And before he took over the first team we had heard from the younger players in the reserves how he had been working with them. They had been impressed and so the dressing-room grapevine had given him a good build-up before he became Boss in November.

In fact, I think the fact that he is almost from the same age group as most of the lads helps him. It is easier to approach him for one thing. I know that when Scot Symon was manager many of the younger boys couldn't pluck up courage to approach him. I don't think he was unapproachable to that extent but he didn't come to the training all the time, and he came from a different generation. I know that when he did watch some of the training games a few of the young lads became so nervous that they couldn't show their real form!

Now this has all changed. The Boss is with us all the time and he can be approached easily. Yet he still maintains discipline. He can be seen without too much trouble. He mixes with the players. He plays in the practice games; yet we all know that we cannot step out of line. And we have enough respect for him not to do so.

After one league game last year against Hibs at Easter Road when we won 3–1, we had to go back to Largs to prepare for the match with Leeds the following week. That night, because we had had a good result he came with us into the hotel bar and bought us a few lagers, something that had been unheard of before. That's the sort of thing that brings him closer to the players and takes us closer to him.

You feel, all the time, that he is ready to talk things over with you, to listen to your point of view. At team discussions he doesn't lay down his ideas in any inflexible way. He likes everyone to say what they feel about his views, not simply accept them. He realises that any one of the lads might have a valid point to bring up and the chance is always there for anyone to do so.

I remember before the Cologne game in Germany he was quite straightforward with us. He told us bluntly: 'This is the first time I have been abroad in charge of a team. I know it is nothing new for you as players so I'm ready to listen to any ideas you have. I know what I want to do, how I want to play the game but you have been through all this as players and if you can help me with suggestions then I'll be listening...'

We respected that. And we gave him as much information as we could, as many of our own ideas and views as we could. Yet, in the end, all of them meant nothing within twenty-five seconds of the game starting.

All the talk we had had about playing it tight for the first twenty minutes was wiped out when the opposition scored that first goal. Yet the Boss had listened to us and learned, and in the end he learned more from that one game than any of us could possibly have told him. He learned then about the uncertainty of European football, how every plan can collapse around you when you go to the Continent to play one of these vital European ties.

Yet he brought us into these talks more than before. He is a players' manager, always trying to do something to help the lads, trying to get us the benefits he feels we deserve. Above all he believes that as members of Rangers we are top players and that we must be treated that way and we must behave in a manner befitting our status.

In seven months he managed to swing every player solidly behind him. We were desperately disappointed when the league was lost and the disappointment we felt was for the Boss as much as for the fans and ourselves.

We want to bring success back to the club for him as well as for anyone else now. It is often said that a manager who gets the backing of his players is halfway along the road to success . . . Davie White is there now.

9

Two Fairs' Cup victories

WE HAD FAILED the previous season, not only in Nuremberg, but at home, too. We had failed to win the league title after chasing Celtic until the second last match of the Scottish season and a few months before that we had suffered our biggest-ever Cup disaster... defeat at Berwick by the tiny Second Division team Berwick Rangers.

That 1–0 Cup defeat at Shielfield Park was easily the worst Scottish Cup result in Ibrox history. Nothing like it had ever happened before. In England top clubs have been knocked out of the Cup by 'rabbits' and these occasional freak results are accepted. But in Scotland this was something that was almost unbelievable, a once in a lifetime event and I had to be the man who skippered Rangers that gloomy afternoon.

That result kept us from winning the Cup and repeating the victory of the season before when we had beaten Celtic after a Hampden replay. And it also led to our two main strikers, Jim Forrest and George McLean, leaving the club. Forrest was transferred to Preston North End and McLean went to Dundee in exchange for Andy Penman. They were transferred because we had missed chances that would have won us the game, chances that would probably have been taken if the team had been properly keyed up for the game. Unhappily I think that all the boys felt the same as the supporters—that we would win easily, and so we took it far too leisurely.

Little Sammy Reid scored Berwick's goal at a time when we were throwing everything into attack in the second half and they had packed their defence. Though I must admit they might have snatched another goal as we neglected defence in a desperate effort to score. Willie Johnston broke an ankle that day and Davy Wilson came on as a substitute but no team changes would have made any difference... we were beaten by that time. The Johnston injury blow capped a day of disaster, a day that no one will ever forget. I only wish they would....

Anyway, without a league or a Cup victory we won only a place in the number three European tournament, the Fairs Cities' Cup. I say 'number three tournament' because it is always rated behind the European Cup and the Cup Winners' Cup but I know that many people rate it almost as highly as the main tourney, the European Cup. They reckon that the teams in the Fairs Cities are very often the best teams in the various countries at the time the games are being played, whereas the teams in the European Cup are the champions of the previous season.

I can understand the point of view. When we played Leeds United they were being rated the finest team in England, ahead of the European Cup representatives Manchester United. And I saw the Hungarian champions, Ferencvaros, the team who will represent Hungary in next year's European Cup, playing Liverpool in a Fairs Cup game just a couple of weeks after clinching their own domestic title.

This was the first time we had played in the Fairs Cup.

But Alex Smith and Alex Ferguson the two players who had been bought for £50,000 and £60,000 from Dunfermline had plenty of experience with the Fife club in the competition. They told us that often you could find yourselves playing fairly easy teams in the opening rounds...then suddenly, bang!—you were in the big-time, facing some of the best teams in Europe!

The draw for the first round was made in Frankfurt just before our season started and our manager at that time, Scot Symon, was there when we were drawn against the East German team Dynamo Dresden. We thought when we got that news that Alex and 'Fergie' had been right, that the easy draw had come up. The last time Rangers had played an East German team had been about six years previously in the European Cup. On that occasion the opposition had been the Berlin team Vorwaerts and we had won 3–1 in Berlin. That game gave me my first trip abroad with the team. I was a young reserve taken along for experience and I felt that the experience would help me now.

I had been a reserve at that game and I remembered the match vividly. The East Germans, on that occasion, had been amateurish in their approach. There had been no sparkle, no imagination in their play and they had looked only half-trained compared with our players. It was a game that Rangers won comfortably and to do that in a European Cup match away from home is unusual, to say the least. So, naturally, my memory of East German football was not one that worried me. I think that the manager felt the same although he stressed to us that no game in Europe could be considered an easy occasion.

My memory and my opinions were scrapped very quickly when we flew there for the match at the start of September. We left Glasgow just two days after we had beaten Celtic in the Ibrox league game, flying to Copenhagen and then direct to East Berlin, finishing the journey to Dresden by coach.

In the game against Celtic Davie Provan had broken a leg and because of that I had been moved to left-back and Davie Smith had taken over as 'sweeper' in the team re-shuffle. When we went to play that first-leg game at the Heinz Steyer Stadium in Dresden the manager decided to stick to this makeshift formation. I am afraid it was not too successful. Instead of coasting to victory against the part-time men of Dresden we found ourselves fighting desperately to return home with a draw. That didn't happen simply because our formation didn't work out. It happened because in six years the game in East Germany had been transformed. The approach to the game had become professional. The players were fitter, better trained and their tactical understanding had developed too. I was surprised—and the other lads were as well.

For long spells in the game we were forced back on defence and at half-time we were lucky to be level 0–0. After the interval Alex Ferguson scored a goal to put us into the lead— a goal that was against the run of play. Eventually the East Germans equalised in the sixty-sixth minute through their outside-right Reidel. From then on we defended with our new goalkeeper Erik Sorensen, the Danish star we had signed from Morton at the start of the season, in magnificent form. He saved us from defeat that afternoon and from what would have turned out to be a very, very hard job in the return game at Ibrox to get through to the second round.

As it was we still had a formidable task even with a draw to help us. There were 52,000 people at the second game to watch the German team which showed some changes. But their danger men, the link man Hoffmann and the outside-left Gumz were both playing.

Their coach Manfred Fuchs had expected to be beaten

over the two games. But the result he got at home and the display his team had given made him more confident. He felt now that his players were not going to be outclassed. He knew there was going to be no disgrace and so his team were able to settle quickly against us and, in fact, they played with more confidence than they had in Dresden.

While they had this settled approach we had been involved in another team switch. Our manager had made up his mind that I could not stay at left-back, that he wanted my drive in midfield. So young Billy Mathieson came in at full-back, Dave Smith stayed alongside Ronnie McKinnon in the centre of the defence and I was made link man along with Andy Penman. I did feel rather out of things at full-back, as I've explained, so I was ready to move.

In the first quarter of an hour we took the lead through Andy Penman and then the Germans closed things up with their giant centre-half Sammer and their veteran skipper Pfeifer commanding their penalty area. There was scarcely a way to get past them and though we battered away at them in attack after attack we failed to score again and clinch the tie. With just a minute left the danger we had worried about, the danger that is always there when you have only a one goal lead, became reality when their inside-forward Kreische scored the equaliser.

That was it. We were in trouble, big trouble, being held to a draw on our own ground by a team of part-time players. No matter how good the part-time players were that was the way the fans looked at them, as players who only played football when their jobs allowed them (even though we knew that under the new East German set-up most of the Dresden players trained as hard and as often as we did). But it was at this time, this time of crisis, that the move which took me into the midfield paid off. We knew how little time there was left. When things are tight you always keep an eye on the dug-out when you can, trying to find out how long there is to go. We reckoned there were only minutes, maybe even seconds to do something, something that would stop the game heading into extra time. We didn't want that. We wanted through to the next round and we powered into a last desperate attack, a last effort to save the game. And we did it. I scored a goal and we were through.

For a moment, however, we didn't realise that the goal had come in time. The referee blew his whistle and then walked to the centre of the field. We didn't know if the ball had gone in before time-up or whether the final whistle had beaten us. Then one of the boys asked him and we realised that we were through. The tension that built up in that moment while we wondered and waited was unbelievable, as unbelievable as the ending to the game, the ending we had wanted, but thought we had missed.

We were through and the second-round draw sent us back to Germany, this time to West Germany and a game against Cologne. This was the team bossed by the veteran German coach Willi Multhaup, the man who had master-minded our old rivals Borussia Dortmund in their victory over Liverpool in the European Cup Winners' Cup Final at Hampden.

Multhaup had European experience behind him and he had as his right-hand man another person with experience, Hans Schafer who had been outside-left in the West German team that won the World Cup in Switzerland in 1954. The team also had in their side three of the current West German international stars, inside-forward Wolfgang Overath, wing-half Wolfgang Weber and centre-forward Johannes Lohr. It promised to be a tough game but then we had experience against German teams and we were ready to face them at any time. We had slammed in five goals against Eintracht Frankfurt in a pre-season game at Ibrox and so we didn't fear Cologne all that much.

Once again though, things changed for us before the second round tie was played. Our manager Scot Symon was dismissed, the team coach Bobby Seith left the club and eventually became manager of Preston North End and our new boss Davie White, who had been assistant manager for several months, took over the team. It was a hard time for him to step into the job. His appointment was announced less than a week before we were due to meet Cologne at Ibrox and he had not seen the Germans in action at all. Spying on our opponents had been done by Mr Symon and Bobby Seith.

Messrs Symon and Seith had watched Cologne in a German league game a few weeks before in preparation for the Fairs' Cup game. Now we were left without guidance from the men who had studied our opponents. Bobby Seith did leave his notes for the new manager but it's always better to see the opposition for yourself and we knew that the new Boss would have liked it that way. Still, we knew that once again, with or without a personal run-down on Cologne, this was a game we had to win. What we wanted to do was to stay in Europe as well as keep ahead of Celtic in the league race. Europe was as important as the league at this stage of the season.

When Cologne arrived they were without the star of the World Cup Final, Weber, because of an injury he received in a game before they flew to Glasgow. The injury to a defender didn't make too much difference to them that night at Ibrox ... because every one of them became defenders! They played as much in defence as Borussia Dortmund had done when they had met Liverpool under Multhaup's guidance. For forty-five minutes, while the 54,000 fans waited patiently, we found our attacks breaking down on the white wall the Germans threw across their eighteen yards' line. While the pressure went on our own defence was having its easiest time for weeks. Cologne were not interested in attacking, only in defending, only in stopping us scoring with the idea of taking us to their own Mungersdorff Stadium to win the tie.

However, our new Boss made one or two changes in our approach when we went in at half-time; he suggested a couple of ideas and before the end we scored three goals. Alex Ferguson got the first, Willie Henderson the second and then, after I had limped off with a strained muscle, "Fergie" got another. We were three goals ahead and confident that we would get through the second leg without too much trouble. We should have known better!

We were warned before going to Cologne that things could be tough. Andy Penman had played against the Germans five years before in a European Cup game for Dundee. The Dens Park team had gone there with a *seven*-goal lead and had almost lost it. That was the hardest game, and the roughest game, that Andy could ever remember playing in. We were warned that we could expect it to be as hard for us because Cologne were upset at losing by three goals and wanted revenge.

They almost got it too. It was an amazing match, a match where we lost three goals, just one less than we had lost in five away games in Europe the year before in our Cup Winners' Cup run, yet I felt that in Cologne we played as well as we had ever played in European football before. In Dortmund against Borussia we had had our backs to the wall and been able to get through to the next round. Here it had been different. We had gone into the game to play in a 4–3–3 set-up that Davie White wanted us to operate for this match. He didn't want all-out defence because he felt—as we all did—that we could hold Cologne without playing that type of game.

We did achieve this in the end but it was as close a finish as we had had in that opening round game against Dresden. It went that way because after just twenty-five seconds' play

Celtic boss Jock Stein, then managing Scotland, greets Rangers' skipper John Greig on the Hampden touchline after he had scored against Italy in the World Cup

Trouble in the match against Borussia in the European Cup Winners game at Ibrox after Greig had been involved in an incident with the German 'keeper

Scotland skipper John Greig heads a Jackie Charlton header over
the bar at Wembley on the day that Scotland beat the World
Champions

Scotland's 'keeper Simpson dives at Alan Ball's feet to make a
save in the England *v* Scotland match at Wembley in 1967

Denis Law tries an overhead kick. George Cohen goes up with
him as Bobby Charlton watches on during the England *v* Scotland
match at Wembley

A royal day for the Old Firm . . . as Scotland captain John Greig
introduces Princess Alexandra to Tommy Gemmell of Celtic

The Rangers Football Club, 1967. Back Row (left to right): Manager Scot Symon, Watson, Provan, McKinnon, Sorenson, Martin, Ritchie, Hynd, Jardine, Persson, and trainer Bobby Seith. Front Row (left to right): Assistant manager Davie White, Henderson, A. Smith, Willoughby, Ferguson, Greig, D. Smith, Penman, Johanson, Johnson, and physiotherapist Davie Kinnear

Cologne scored a goal when a defensive mistake allowed Overath in to cut back our first-leg lead to two goals. For a spell after that we had to hang on as the Germans piled on amazing pressure that had us reeling. We held out though and before half-time we had settled to the pattern of play the Boss had outlined for us before the match. We began to play neat football, the ball was moved around well and we started to dictate the way the game should run. After half-time we kept that up and Cologne were the team in trouble. We were coasting comfortably to victory when we were hit by a two-goal burst and the lead we had brought with us had gone.

The German sweeper Weber came upfield into attack to get the first with just a quarter of an hour left to play and four minutes later a bad decision from the Italian referee, Concetto Lo Bello, allowed them to score the second goal. Our goalkeeper Erik Sorensen started to roll the ball out to avoid taking more than the three steps allowed in the new rule governing goalkeepers carrying the ball and was penalised for wasting time, that was what the referee told us. The free kick inside our penalty box was forced into the net by Ruhl. Fireworks were being let off on the terracings, rockets soared into the sky, the game was level and we were facing defeat. There we were on their ground with eleven minutes left and then the extra half hour if the game was still a draw at the end of ninety minutes. All the advantages, the advantages that we had come with, had moved to them. . . .

That game showed me once again that nothing can be counted as certain in football, especially in European football. You can go into a match confident of victory and then, even though you are playing well, find yourself in trouble. That is what had happened to us. But where many teams would have collapsed we came through. We were fitter and stronger than the Germans and even on their ground we dominated that session of extra time when they should have been taking the initiative. With time running out on us and the horrors of tossing a coin to decide the game looming up in front of me again we got the goal that gave us victory. Willie Henderson scored it with a great shot and the wee man turned cartwheels all the way back to the centre line as our own fans in the crowd gave out with their own verbal fireworks. It was another close thing, the way we seemed to do things all the way through last season, but we were in the next round and that was all that mattered. Though I felt, too, that we deserved praise for the way the team had come back. The manner of our victory, winning when all the odds had moved against us, had been impressive.

Cologne should have been able to win that game. I know that if the positions had been reversed, if we had been playing extra time against them at Ibrox and they had been demoralised by losing a three-goal lead then we would have clinched it in the half-hour extra.

From that point of view it was a good performance. Just as I thought it was a good display from the other point of view too, from the fact that we had gone abroad without playing a game totally committed to defence, that we had played good football, at times attractive football, and done it the way the new manager wanted it.

Only bad luck stopped us getting through the game without the necessity of extra time, bad luck that would have killed most teams, bad breaks that would have meant defeat for most teams. We were able to recover. We had the guts, the stamina and the ability to get the goal that mattered....

That's why, for me, the Cologne performance was as good as any we've given in Europe.

10

Out to Leeds United

WE HAD a breather in Europe after that game in Cologne because in the draw for the next round of the Fairs Cup we were given a bye into the quarter-finals. That bye gave me my first chance to become a soccer spy, a job that I did twice for Rangers last season and a job that I enjoyed doing. Twice I was sent to watch opposition teams, or possible opposition teams, in action because the Boss could not go himself.

The first occasion was when Liverpool played the crack Hungarian team Ferencvaros at Anfield in a second-leg match just before the draw was being made for the quarter-finals. The Boss was in hospital for a minor operation and I was sent south with trainer Davie Kinnear.

It was winter and the pitch at Anfield was covered with more than an inch of snow, but that did nothing to help Bill Shankly's team. They lost 1–0 and they had already been 1–0 down from the first leg in Budapest. That sent them out of the tournament and for my money the Hungarians became the team to fear. And I saw a new Hungarian star, a slim young inside-forward called Zoltan Varga who gave Liverpool's giant defenders Tommy Smith and Ronnie Yeats a miserable night. Ferencvaros were never in any danger yet they were playing without two of their stars, the sweeper Matrai and the incomparable centre-forward Florian Albert.

Davie Kinnear and I were at that match because we *might* be drawn to play against the winners, that's the way the Boss believes in working. Even though we may not necessarily be playing against a certain team, he likes to have them all watched in advance so that we are never caught without some knowledge of the opposition. It was for this reason that he had gone south twice on a previous occasion to watch Leeds United, and these trips paid off when we were eventually drawn to meet them in a quarter-final game which was hailed as a British championship match. At that time both ourselves and Leeds were leading our First Division tables.

But, though he had seen Leeds himself, the Boss believed in being thorough and I was sent south to watch them again. This time I knew that it was an important job, more important than the Anfield visit because this time I was watching our next opponents. This was the team we had to defeat to reach the semi-finals of the Fairs Cities' Cup.

I was suspended for seven days after collecting three cautions and was forced to miss a game at Ibrox against St Johnstone. That gave me my chance to see Leeds in action in the League Cup Final at Wembley against Arsenal. I travelled south with one of the directors, Mr David Hope, and we watched one of the dullest games that has ever graced Wembley. Leeds scored a goal through left-back Terry Cooper halfway through the first half and made up their minds that they were not going to lose this lead.

They had been close so often to winning a major honour and had failed; now they had decided that there would be no slip-ups. No mistakes were going to rob them of their first trophy. It was a dull game to watch but for me it was a good thing because I was able to see the two faces of Leeds United —the attacking face in that opening spell when they were looking for goals, trying to create the scoring chances needed to win the match, and the defensive face, when they dropped back to stop Arsenal snatching their glory away from them. The defensive face was the more impressive, for when Leeds drop back there are few teams who can find a way past that defence.

When I am asked to spy on a team the first thing I look for is the basic playing pattern, whether they play 4–2–4 or 4–3–3, who the link men are and the providers and the strikers, the key men in the tactical formation. These are the main points to watch when you are taking your first look at a team. Then you move on to the individual players, pinpointing the main danger men and watching for any weaknesses that your own team may be able to exploit. They may be guilty of playing a certain type of ball the same way every time, or beating a man the same way when they are moving forward with the ball.

Many players don't like watching a game when they are not playing. I know that Denis Law hates sitting in the stand watching a match when he is off with an injury and Willie Henderson is the same. But I enjoy going to watch a match, especially when it is a game where I am going to be learning something that will help me in the future.

In this game I was getting a first-hand look at the tactics which would be used against us when we came to play Leeds and I had to try to get some idea how we could beat that defence, and also how we could counter any of the attacking moves that Leeds had. Largely, this meant that we had to have some ideas on how to deal with their dead ball moves.

Anyone who watches Leeds must be impressed by the way they use corners and free kicks. They have got this down to a fine art, probably better than any other team I've seen. They have moves at corner kicks which involved big Jack Charlton coming upfield to worry the opposition goalkeeper, and at free kicks they have other moves involving other players which can cause any team and any defence big trouble. They get a lot of vital goals from these moves and I realised that we would have to have something ready to use against them, some plans of our own to combat these Leeds moves.

Naturally, the Boss had had the same views as myself after watching them earlier in the season. But he didn't ask me about my opinion of Leeds or what I thought our approach to the games should be until much nearer the time we were set to play against them. Then, at a team talk he asked me to give my ideas on the opposition. Our views coincided on a lot of points. We had both thought we had spotted weaknesses that we would be able to play on when the games took place.

I felt, for instance, that the Leeds' full-backs, Paul Reaney and Terry Cooper, were good attacking players, fast and very dangerous when they were coming forward with the ball. But I also thought that if they were faced with two wingers who would be ready to take them on then they wouldn't look nearly so good. In fact, in the second game at Leeds when Willie Henderson hit form that was proved right because Terry Cooper had no idea how to stop him. The Boss agreed here and he had his own ideas on how to combat the Leeds set-piece moves at frees and corners. Apart from the penalty—and that cannot count—they had no success against us with these moves.

The man we tried to take out of the two games was little Irishman Johnny Giles. In the League Cup Final at Wembley everything had stemmed from him, all the Leeds moves had been set up by him, every exciting attack they made was started by him. He is a wonderfully accurate passer of the ball and can make space for himself almost uncannily. Johnny never seems to get possession of the ball when he is marked. He is always on his own, ready to set some move up before the opposition can pin him down. We wanted this stopped in the games against us and again we were successful. For although we were beaten over the two matches Johnny was never able to take control the way he so often does in the games Leeds play in England.

These things worked for us yet we still lost. It seems strange but that is the way it is when you come up against Leeds United. They always seem to have some alternative, some other way of beating the other team. They have a tremendous team understanding built up at Elland Road, a spirit that has everyone working for everyone else all the time. That's what allows them to hit you unexpectedly when you think you have their number one danger man bottled up. We also lost because we missed chances over the two games, just as we had done the previous season. This time we had been able to set up more chances, able to create more match-winning opportunities but the old failing in front of goal haunted us once more. We failed to score at Ibrox and we failed again at Elland Road and when you do that you cannot win games. It's as simple as that....

In the no-scoring draw at Ibrox we knew we should have scored goals and we knew that when we didn't score at home we faced a tough fight. Somehow though we still felt we could get to the semi-finals. In the Fairs' Cup tournament with away goals counting double in the event of a draw we knew that a draw at Elland Road would take us through... unless the score remained at 0–0 when the toss of a coin would decide.

Knowing that we were ready to have a go when we went to Leeds and we did just that. Leeds' skipper Billy Bremner admitted to me afterwards that his team had never known a harder opening twenty minutes in any game they had played

at Elland Road that season. He admitted that in that spell of
Rangers' pressure he had thought that they were going to
lose the tie.

Then in the twenty-fifth minute after Alex Ferguson, back
defending, had handled after a Johnny Giles corner kick,
the penalty was converted. Seven more minutes and the game
was over. Jimmy Greenhoff mishit a shot for goal and it
landed at Peter Lorimer's feet for the Dundee-born boy to
put them two in front with a hard, low shot.

We wondered then just what we had to do to beat this
team. We went on trying, we still managed to regain control
until half-time and then after the interval Leeds took over.
That two-goal lead gave them the confidence they needed to
throw off the effects of our power opening and from then on
we knew that we were not going to win this one. Leeds had
regained all their composure and we realised that this team
would not make two mistakes, that their defence was too well-
drilled to make the errors that we needed to give us victory.
Looking back at that tie I sometimes wonder what might
have happened if Willie Johnston had scored with a chance
he had after two minutes. That would have put us ahead at
a time when Billy Bremner told me that his team were under
more pressure than they had experienced against anyone else
that year. I think that could have made all the difference,
that could have meant victory for us, but we missed the
chance and that's that.

If you can't score goals then you don't deserve victory, we
learned that the hard way last season at Leeds, just as we
had learned it at Nuremberg a few months before. Still,
though that was the main reason for our defeat I don't want
to detract from Leeds United's victory. Their manager Don
Revie has built them into one of the finest teams we have ever
played against in Europe. Saragossa were a better footballing
team, a more open team to come up against, a more attrac-

tive team to watch but I would play them before I would play Leeds United any day. In fact, I would play most teams in Europe before I would tackle Leeds in a two-leg knock-out tourney. They have become one of the most difficult teams in Europe to beat in these competitions.

Yet, because I am stressing how hard they are to beat don't run away with the impression that Leeds are simply a defensive team. There is more to this Yorkshire team than that. In midfield Billy Bremner and Johnny Giles have as much footballing skill and ability as any midfield players with any team anywhere. Behind them Norman Hunter plays the double centre-half role as well as any player I've played against. He tackles powerfully, he reads the game well, and he can move out of his defensive role to use the ball with intelligence and imagination. Maybe the forward four aren't as big stars as the men I have mentioned but they possess the driving ambition that consumes this team. That to Leeds United is as important as anything else. They don't want a moody genius up front who will give them ten minutes work in a game. They want players who will run for them all day, work for them as hard as they know how, and players who will do exactly what is demanded of them by manager Don Revie. That's what they've got right now.

Given another year or two, providing they can steer clear of serious injuries, I think Leeds can become one of the best teams in the world. They have the basis of a truly great team there at Elland Road now. All they need is a little more time to develop individual skills and no one will be able to touch them. As it is few teams can! Strangely, though, they are criticised for not being attractive enough to watch. In the League Cup Final they were dull. I admit that. But they had a job to do and they did it successfully. I think that the flair and imagination that some people feel they lack will come over the next few seasons. They showed in that second half against us at Elland Road that they can play football and turn on the style when the occasion is there for it.

Watching Billy Bremner playing for Leeds is a revelation to anyone who has only seen him in a Scotland jersey. He does a different job for his club than he does for his country. He is used solely as an attacking wing-half, not in the marking role or the sweeper role that he has been used in for Scotland. He is a better player for Leeds, not because he gives more effort, no one can give more effort for his country than little Billy, but because he is allowed to express himself more. He is given more freedom in the Leeds side than he usually gets from Scotland. Some day he will get his club role for Scotland and that will open everyone's eyes!

Billy isn't just the tough tackling, quick-tempered little red-head that so many people think of. He is a highly skilled player as well, something that too many fans tend to forget, just as they forget the skilful qualities of the Leeds United team.

The two games against Leeds and conversations I had with Billy Bremner after the games convinced me once again that what we need more than anything else is the chance to play against top English teams more regularly. In Scotland, and I include Celtic here, we tend to play quite a number of matches every season where the result is a foregone conclusion. Games take place some Saturdays when no one can really expect either of the Old Firm teams to slip up and this is bad training for the challenges of European football. There can be spells in a season when the edge can go off the team a little because the quality of the opposition does not have players on their toes all the time. I know that teams can raise their games when they meet ourselves or Celtic but they can't raise it to match the standard of play that teams like Leeds meet in England week after week.

Last year Leeds were in the running for every major

honour when we played them. They had won the League Cup just before we met them, were leading the English League and in the semi-finals of the English Cup. Yet Bremner and some of the other players told us that there was never a single game where they could relax a little, where a win was a certainty.

Billy pointed out to me that there were teams struggling against relegation in England who had an awful lot of talent, West Ham was one team in this category. In Scotland we don't have this quality right through the league competition. We need more games with a real challenge and then we can prepare properly for the extra that is asked in European tournaments. It's no use playing a team that is struggling badly in our First Division one Saturday then playing Real Madrid or Benfica or Leeds United a few days later. Where is the preparation in that? What kind of test do we really get? We may drop a point because they mass in defence, for, remember a bad team can often pack their penalty box as efficiently as a good team! Yet that still doesn't get you in the right frame of mind to take on the top teams from other European countries where, very often, the leagues are of a higher standard.

I am not talking about the top of our league here, by the way. I'm talking really about the last half-dozen clubs or so. Clubs who rarely, if ever, manage to defeat either member of the Old Firm.

In England you are always meeting teams who are coming out to play with fresh ideas, new tactics, plans that have been laid specifically to defeat you and you have got to be able to find an answer to these moves. That way you keep in step with the latest developments in football. Your ideas aren't allowed to become set and old-fashioned. In Scotland a packed defence is the most that some of the poorer teams can

offer and even then, power and better training take you
through if superior ability fails.

In England that doesn't happen because every team is fit
and well-trained, as fit as Leeds or Liverpool or Manchester
United or Spurs. They don't crumble in front of the big
names down there so that every week becomes a week where
you have to play hard and think hard to get the victories
needed to win honours.

We need that in Scotland too. That would help us in
Europe. At the moment we have pre-season games and sometimes other friendlies, and all of them teach us something.
When you play Spurs and Arsenal—our opponents at the
start of this season—you get something from each team that
you can use.

More opportunities like these are what we all want. . . .

11

Old Firm rivalry

THE LEAGUE race last season ended on the very last
day...and once again we had lost the title to our 'Old Firm'
rivals, Celtic. It was the third year in a row that they had won
the championship and the second year in a row that we had
been beaten at the last gasp.

But this time it was harder to take than ever before because
for the whole season, right until the second last match of the
year we had led the way, perhaps occasionally slipping back
into second place because we had a game in hand...but
always the team best placed to take the title. Always the team
who were favourites to become champions. Then disaster
struck us, just as it had struck so many teams when they are
trying to go for all the honours. Instead of going on to win
the title, lift the Scottish Cup and take the Fairs Cities' Cup
we lost every single one inside the space of a couple of months.

The Scottish Cup defeat from Hearts came first when we
were beaten by the only goal in a Tynecastle replay. From
that game on the team did not play as well as it had been
doing. Little things started going wrong, the strain began to

tell on some of the lads, the rhythm of our earlier performances wasn't there any more.

And to add to all that worry Andy Penman went down
with illness just at the time he was hitting top form.

In addition, we had Willie Johnston losing form. Until he
was chosen to play for Scotland against England at Hampden
Willie had been the deadliest striker in the country. Then
on February 24, in that international match, Willie had a
bad game and the gnawing doubts that can eat away at a
striker's confidence hit him when we needed him—and his
goals—most.

Yet, even with all these problems we should still have
won the title. It was one of the most bitter disappointments
of my life when we lost and because of the way we lost.

But the story of the title wasn't just the story of the last
few games, it was, as always, the story of the whole season,
because it is a season's consistency that eventually pays off
with a place in the European Cup and a league championship flag flying over your ground. At the beginning of the
year, the start of the league race we were the form team. We
felt that we could beat Celtic, even though they had qualified for the League Cup knock-out stages by beating us in
our section. But these games have to be examined and then
you can see the reasons for our own confidence.

That section draw for the League Cup had given the new
season the best send-off possible. The Celtic manager, Jock
Stein, described our section as 'the finest that's ever been
drawn together in the tournament' ... and I wouldn't disagree with that. Few people could.

Celtic were there, we were there, and joining us were the
beaten Scottish Cup Finalists Aberdeen and Dundee United,
the only team who had taken full league points off Celtic
the previous season. It could not have been any harder for a
team to qualify for the quarter-finals and it couldn't have

been more entertaining for the fans. All of us looked forward to it. We wanted to have another crack at Celtic, the new European champions.

Our team had been strengthened again. Andy Penman had come the season before in a swap deal for George McLean but had been signed too late to take part in any of our vital closing matches. Now he was available.

We also had £60,000 centre-forward Alex Ferguson from Dunfermline, the highest-priced player in Scotland after we had bought him. Swedish international outside-left Orjan Persson had come from Dundee United and the Danish goal-keeper Erik Sorensen had been bought from Morton just before the season opened.

It was another massive spending spree by the club, which was determined to overhaul Celtic. Then we lost in our first pre-season match against Arsenal at Highbury. Yet the defeat came mainly because the re-built team was still settling down, the players still getting to know each other. In our second challenge game, against Eintracht Frankfurt, we hit form and slammed in five goals against them at Ibrox. That really set all of us in the right frame of mind for the League Cup challenge we were going to have to face up to against Celtic.

We wanted revenge for the league defeat of the year before. We thought we would get it when we were suddenly hit by a penalty jinx which robbed us of victories over our biggest rivals in both games we played.

The first game was at Ibrox, a mid-week evening game which had 94,000 fans packed into the ground. It was the clash they had all been waiting for since the 2–2 draw which ended the last season.

Again it was close, even closer than that last game we had had. This time Celtic went into the lead in the first half. They scored from a penalty, given for a Dave Smith foul on Bobby Lennox. Tommy Gemmell took the kick and scored.

Then, in the second half, we were given a penalty with half an hour to go. Our new man Andy Penman who had never missed a penalty in all his years with Dundee stepped forward to take it. He had been taking them in practice games because the year before we had had a spate of missed penalties including Dave Smith's in Saragossa. This time, though, Ronnie Simpson saved Andy's shot and we struggled to get another goal to draw. It came just two minutes from the end when Andy made up for that earlier miss by scoring direct from a free kick on the edge of the penalty box. We had had the best of that second half and naturally we all felt that if we had been able to score from the penalty then we would have won the game.

So, even though we had dropped a point at home we were certain we could win the section, that we could beat Celtic at Celtic Park to do this. Our performance had given us that boost even if luck had taken away a good result. . . .

We also felt that we had proved to the new players in the team that Celtic were not invincible. They were European Cup holders, respected all over the world as such, but in an 'Old Firm' game they were simply Glasgow Celtic, a team who were our greatest rivals, a team we respected but, at the same time, a team we had beaten many times in the past.

The thing I felt we had to do was to make the other lads, the new boys, understand that Celtic were not a team that we had to fear. Respect, yes. When I first went into the Rangers' first team I respected Celtic, even though at that time they rarely managed to beat us and had gone close to ten years without a major trophy win. These things didn't count then and there was no reason for the European Cup victory to change that in any way. 'Old Firm' games are something else, something different. They are games where anything can happen—and usually does. Games, too, where form or reputation does not count too much. But, even though I'm always prepared for the dramatic happenings in these games I was not ready for what happened to us in the return clash at Celtic Park a couple of weeks later. Again there was a huge crowd, 75,000 this time, to see the game that would settle the section, that would decide which of us went into the League Cup quarter-finals, and also which of the teams was the best bet for the league title.

This time we were first to take the lead after only nine minutes when Willie Henderson cut inside on to a pass from Andy Penman and scored. It was a dream opening for us and the game stayed that way until fourteen minutes from the end. It was in that seventy-sixth minute that everything was decided. Celtic had been trying to get the equaliser that they needed so much and they were failing. Then we broke clear down the right, and again it was Willie Henderson who was cutting in on goal, ready to shoot when this time he was brought down by John Clark. The referee, Tom Wharton gave a penalty immediately.

We had changed our penalty taker after that miss by Andy Penman at Ibrox and now our right-back Kai Johansen, the man whose goal had given us our last victory over Celtic eighteen months before in the Scottish Cup Final replay, stepped forward to take it.

But the penalty jinx hit us once more. Kai hammered the ball for goal but it was an inch too high and it slammed against the underside of the bar and then bounced down on to the line before Ronnie Simpson could move for it. Kai ran forward to hit the ball into the net, to make certain, but, of course, was penalised when he touched the ball. It was seconds later that we discovered that Kai had thought the ball was over the line when it came down and was hitting it again in celebration. He had gone for the ball thinking the referee had already given a goal and he hit it as Andy Pen-

4—ACP

man came in behind him. If Andy had put the ball in then we would have been in the lead despite the penalty miss.

But, of course, referee Wharton decided that the ball had not crossed the line before Kai touched it the second time. He gave a free kick to Celtic and within a minute they had equalised when Willie Wallace scored after a corner.

Now, instead of being two goals ahead, we had been pulled back to level and as we tried to pull ourselves together Celtic stormed back into the attack. Before the end they scored two more goals through Bobby Murdoch and Bobby Lennox, crashed through into the quarter-finals and, in fact, went on to beat Dundee in the League Cup Final.

We left Celtic Park that night wondering just what we had to do to beat them. Over the whole 180 minutes of these two games they hadn't played any better than us. In fact, we had had the edge. Yet in the end we could only draw one game and lose the other. It was a tragedy for all of us, and, especially for Andy Penman and Kai Johansen, the men whose penalty misses had proved so costly.

In just a few more weeks we realised that we would have to meet Celtic once again in the first league game between the two teams at Ibrox. We knew that this time we would have to win. If we lost then it would give Celtic the edge for the title and that was something that we couldn't afford after that Celtic Park defeat.

Yet, because we had been so close to victory twice we still felt that we could pull it off if only the breaks went for us. Once again though, with 90,000 fans watching, a cruel slice of luck hit us in the first half. Our Scottish international left-back Dave Provan went into a tackle with Bertie Auld, went down awkwardly and was carried off the field with a broken leg. That meant a team re-shuffle, one that took me to left-back and had Dave Smith slot into the sweeper's position alongside centre-half Ronnie McKinnon.

I think that at that moment, as Davie was being taken to the dressing-room, all the bad luck we had had against Celtic that season flooded back into our minds. I doubt if any of us felt at that time that we could change that luck...but we did!

The man who changed it was one of the new signings, the tall, blond Swede Orjan Persson who slashed home a shot just two minutes after the start of the second half. That turned out to be the only goal of the game. One goal was enough to win us the match, end our jinx against our 'Old Firm' rivals and send us into the lead in the league championship race...a lead that was to last until the second last game of the season!

It was an important goal for us for that reason and also for another reason. It proved to everyone that Celtic boss Jock Stein and his players didn't have any Indian sign on us. We continued to prove that in the next league game on January 3 at Celtic Park when we went there and drew 2–2.

This was a controversial game. For a start injuries and suspension to centre-forward Alex Ferguson had forced us into changes, changes that brought accusations of power play against us. They were not true. Roger Hynd was brought in at centre-forward because he was considered the best man to take over from Alex Ferguson and I was moved to left-back because Billy Mathieson had a badly inflamed ankle bone. At the time the Celtic fans claimed that I had been put at left-back as a strong-arm man to stop Jimmy Johnstone. How wrong they were.

If there had been no injury to Mathieson then I would have been playing in midfield as usual and we would have had a better chance of winning the game. I felt that and I know that manager Davie White felt exactly the same way. He gave Billy Mathieson a try-out on the morning of the game and was forced to leave him out at the last minute.

That's when I was moved, in the same switch that had been made when Dave Provan broke a leg in the first game.

After the game the criticism went on because I played the game hard, just the way that I always play. I play to win and I play the type of game that brings physical contact between players, yet I was criticised not only by the Celtic fans but also by the official Celtic newspaper, *The Celtic View*. Even towards the end of the season I was getting letters from Celtic fans, abusive letters and threatening letters about that game, many of them carrying the clipping of *The Celtic View* article condemning my treatment of Jimmy Johnstone.

But in spite of all that I walked off the field together with wee Jimmy at the end and he made no complaint. I get on well with him in the international team get-togethers that we have. I wouldn't say that he thought I'd gone out on to the field to deliberately play dirty against him.

I remember just one bad foul I committed against him in the game and that happened because I had an ankle injury myself that was troubling me. Jimmy put the ball past me. I couldn't turn quickly enough because of the pain in my ankle and as he was going past me I brought him down with my body, not by kicking him. It was a foul that looked a whole lot worse than it was.

It is as well to remember here that in that game I was spoken to by the referee just once. I wasn't booked so I couldn't have been as bad as people made out. I reckon that the whole thing blew up because I had to play against a little fellow and that's something I've always disliked. I've said this before. I remember being asked before a Scotland–England game if I preferred to play against Jimmy Greaves or Roger Hunt. There was no need for a great deal of thought on my part. I named Hunt immediately. I didn't decide that on the question of ability. It's as simple as this—Roger Hunt is a big, strong, powerful player who relishes bodily contact in a

tackle. Greaves, small and slim, doesn't. When I move in to
tackle a smaller player it can look bad but I can't change my
style because of the size of my opponent. That's the way it
was at Celtic Park with Jimmy Johnstone. It's just a hard
job convincing some of the Celtic fans that I'm telling the
truth.

I'm certain of one thing. If they had won the game that
day the Johnstone business would have been forgotten a long
time ago. They were desperately looking for some excuse after
dropping a valuable point to us so they picked on me and
claimed I treated Jimmy Johnstone badly.

I never deny that I'm a hard player. I play that way
because it's the style I've always played. In that sense I
suppose I am a bit like Nobby Stiles of England or Terry
Hennessey of Wales. Hard tackling players, both of them,
something that you have got to be when you are a defensive
wing-half. It is almost essential to be strong and powerful in
the tackle when you are being asked to stop the opposing
strikers.

Anyhow, to get back to that game at Celtic Park. They
had taken the lead in the first half when a Bertie Auld free
kick struck Sandy Jardine and was deflected into the net past
Erik Sorensen. Ten minutes after half-time we got the equaliser when their goalkeeper, John Fallon substituting for the
injured Ronnie Simpson, allowed a shot from Willie Johnston
to go through his legs and into the net. They went ahead
again in seventy-eight minutes when Bobby Murdoch scored
but with three minutes left we snatched a draw when Fallon
mistimed a long-range try from Kai Johansen. The goalkeeping mistakes had allowed us our chance and this time
we had not been careless enough to pass the chance up.

It had been a tense game, even more tense than the others
and there had not been very much good football. But what
mattered to us was that we had kept our lead in the league.

Celtic wanted to win that game, they had to win it. In that
sense the 2–2 draw was a victory for us. We had held Celtic
on their own ground and consolidated our lead at the top of
the First Division table.

From then until the end of the season we knew that we had
to hang on to that lead and we fought as hard as we knew
how to do it. We were tipped to lose in the league game at
Tynecastle against Hearts but we won. We were tipped to
lose at East End Park against Dunfermline but we won again.
We were tipped to lose at Easter Road against Hibs and we
won again with one of our best displays of the season. That
seemed to be it. There didn't seem a single game left that
should cause us much concern. The games left were against
the smaller teams, teams we had already beaten and there
didn't seem one that could cost us the title. But, as usual,
things went wrong for us when we least expected it.

The place that I feel we really lost the title was at Tanna-
dice when we went there to play Dundee United. Earlier in
the season the game had been postponed because of snow.
Now we went to play it at a vital stage of the season. And
what was worse the game came at a time when our form had
started to shade off, when the strain of carrying an unbeaten
league record began to tell on some members of the team.

That night against Dundee United we were held to a 0–0
draw in a game where we had enough chances to win comfortably. Ironically, one of the men who stopped us that
night was my pal and old team-mate Jimmy Millar. Jimmy
had been in our team in the sweeper role when we had
beaten Celtic in the Scottish Cup Final nearly two years
before. Now here he was in the same position playing against
us and playing as efficiently as ever. All the experience Jimmy
had gained in football—most of it at Ibrox with Rangers—
was used now to stop us and to help Celtic in their title bid.
He did it so well that we couldn't score and the two-point

lead we had held over Celtic became just one point, a point that we couldn't afford to lose. For by this time Celtic had a better goal average than we did and losing that solitary point would leave us level on points but in second place on goal average.

The other point was dropped in the second last game of the season when we went to Greenock to play Morton at Cappielow. By this time nothing was coming easy for us; we were scraping home in all our games and because of the difficulty we had in getting goals, everything was being thrown into attack. We played that way at Cappielow and were punished by losing two goals in the first half. We went in at half-time two goals down with defeat looking up for the first time in the league that season.

I got one goal back early in the second half, then Morton scored again. Before the end it took goals from Willie Johnston and myself again to give us a draw. Yet Andy Penman had a shot kicked off the line in the last minute, a shot that would have given us victory and possibly the title, too. For if we had won there our confidence would have returned. Unhappily it wasn't to be.

Celtic were now in the lead by goal average and we both had two games to play. We had Kilmarnock at Rugby Park and Aberdeen at Ibrox while Celtic had Morton at Celtic Park and Dunfermline at East End Park.

It was on that second last day of the season that the drama and the tension became almost unbearable for all of us. We were at Rugby Park, a hard place at any time, and even harder when you are looking for two vital points. We got them by winning 2–1 with a goal from Alex Willoughby clinching things halfway through the second half. Then we went into the dressing-room, anxiously waiting to hear the Celtic score against Morton. We were given it as 1–1 and the fans still inside the ground had the same score broadcast to them. The celebrations started right away. Thousands of our supporters danced over the Rugby Park turf chanting 'Champions...champions..." They sang and they cheered and in the bath we were just as deliriously happy as they were.

Then, in the middle of it all, we were given the correct score from Celtic Park...2–1 for Celtic. And all the dreams we had had of the title were killed, all the hopes that Celtic had at last slipped were finished.

It turned out that they had scored a goal in injury time, that little Bobby Lennox had squeezed the ball over the line when the game was two minutes over the regulation ninety. It was the lateness of the goal that had caused the mix-up at Rugby Park and made us feel worse than at any other time during the season.

To get the score that way, to have all our high hopes come tumbling down around us in the middle of celebrating was the worst blow of all. I think that right there and then we all knew that we would lose the title no matter what happened in our final league game at Ibrox against Aberdeen. All of us seemed to know that Celtic would not slip up against Dunfermline, a team who were playing in the Scottish Cup Final just three days before that last league match.

As it happened that Dunfermline clash didn't matter at all. We lost our last game 3–2 to Eddie Turnbull's team after holding the lead twice. This time it was our turn to experience the disaster of goalkeeping mistakes and all that they can mean to a team. Erik Sorensen let two bad goals past him—he admitted it himself after the game—and we lost and gave Celtic the title while they were sitting in the Hampden stand watching the Cup Final.

Celtic had won the title on goal average and though they eventually won against Dunfermline, too, that didn't matter. They were the champions again.

The end at Hampden last year and Scotland's European Nations Cup hopes die as Greig (6) holds out his hand to England's Martin Peters

Captains John Greig and Bobby Moore come out on to the field before the vital game between Scotland and England at Hampden

The first disaster at Berwick when Norrie Martin is beaten by the Sammy Reid shot which sent Rangers to their worst ever defeat in the Scottish Cup first round

Second disaster at Berwick when Willie Johnston is laid on a stretcher with a serious ankle injury. Skipper Greig and Alex Smith are the two Rangers beside the stretcher

Preparing at Largs for the Leeds game are (left to right) Alex Smith, Greig, Alec Willoughby, Sandy Jardine and Willie Johnston

Training before Nuremberg with former Manager Scot Symon on the left. Leading the training run are (left to right) Davy Wilson, Greig, Willie Henderson and Billy Ritchie

The last trophy win in 1967—and the only one so far under Greig's captaincy. Kai Johansen (left) and Dave Provan crown Greig with the Scottish Cup. On the extreme left is George McLean

John Greig in a special action pose at Ibrox, as he tries to bring down a difficult high ball

The results at the end of the season had cost us the title. Yet even now it is an amazing fact that if we had won against Aberdeen and gone right through our league programme undefeated we would still have lost the title. That is the level of the competition now between ourselves and Celtic at the top. To win the championship Celtic had to build up a record number of points and the gap between the top two teams and the third team, Hibs, was sixteen points.

Yet that didn't count for our fans. They stood outside and jeered the players as they left after that solitary league defeat. I wasn't one of their victims but I still felt it was wrong of them to do that to any of the lads. Everyone had tried. Everyone had wanted the title just as much as the fans did. No one deliberately set out to let Celtic win, no one in particular let the team down. Things just went wrong for us.

And I think it was in these angry scenes at the last game that several of the new players realised just what it means to be a Rangers player. They learned just how much our fans demand of us in a season. With other clubs it is an achievement to be second in the league, and more of an achievement to go so long unbeaten. With Glasgow Rangers to be second —especially to Celtic—is failure.

Erik Sorensen was sitting on his own in the dressing-room after that Aberdeen match when I went over to him. I tried to tell him not to worry too much and he said : 'I know now what it means to play for Rangers. I have learned it the hard way.'

This is something that you experience only in great success or failure. I remember when I found out what it is to play for Rangers and it was in very different circumstances. It was back in June 1962 when we flew back from a three-game tour of Russia when the team had been unbeaten. Ten thousand fans swarmed around the aircraft as it landed. They broke down the barriers and charged across the tarmac to welcome us. And to welcome me for the first time. Because that was the first time I had been one of the first team men who were being saluted.

Ten days earlier I had left Scotland unknown, then I was chosen to play in all three games as a wing-half deputy for Jim Baxter who was touring with an Army team. That tour took me into the first team and turned me into a wing-half after I had spent most of my career at inside-forward. But that night at Renfrew Airport I learned what Erik Sorensen learned after the Aberdeen match, what it means to play for Rangers.

If we had won the league Erik would have learned it the same way as I did—in success with every player a king in his own right. But with Rangers the distance between kings and beggars is just a finger-tip . . . we knew that for the second year in a row!

12

The way ahead

AFTER THESE two seasons of bitter disappointment I've made a vow to myself that I won't make any predictions about how Rangers are going to do in Scottish football.

I've felt for two seasons—and I've said so, too—that we would break through to win at least one of the major honours. Then last year, with the two top honours, the Scottish Cup and the league, there to be won, and especially the league, we lost them both.

It was a disastrous setback to all of us and for two years in succession we had failed to win any of Scotland's top trophies. For our last victory—and the only one under my captaincy of the team—you have to go back to the Scottish Cup Final two years ago. That was the game when we were written off before the start, yet went on to beat Celtic in the replay by a Kai Johansen goal.

All this would be easier to take, I suppose, if we were losing the main honours to other teams instead of to Celtic. But with the set-up the way it is in Scotland, the rivalry between the two clubs and the two sets of supporters, it makes

it almost unbearable. When I first took over the team captaincy I used to feel that I wanted to lift these trophies for the
sake of the supporters, now I desperately want to win them for
myself. I want to know what it means to win these honours
just as I did when I first came into the Rangers team as a
youngster.

That Rangers team, the one I virtually learned my trade
in, lined up this way: Ritchie; Shearer, Caldow; Greig,
McKinnon, Baxter; Henderson, McMillan, Millar, Brand,
Wilson. And that was a team that swept the boards in one
great season in Scotland, just as Celtic did the other year. It
was a fine team, a team that had as its main difference between it and the present team the fact that every member of
that forward line could score goals. It didn't seem to matter
who the ball ran to, or how it ran to them, they all had the
knack of being able to stick it in the back of the net. But,
as everyone knows, we have had a goal-scoring problem these
last two seasons. I feel that we are creating as many chances
today as we did then, and I think that the defence is probably better than it was then, but now we just fail in front
of goal.

That is the difference as I see it between those two Rangers
teams and it is also the difference between our team and
Celtic right now. I think that we are just a shade off being a
great team, just a fraction away from being as good a team
as Celtic are. Their victory in the European Cup proved to
everyone how great they were, especially when you consider
the quality of the opposition they met on the way to that
Lisbon final. Teams like Vojvodina and Dukla Prague are
in the very top bracket of European soccer. Celtic beat them
both.

Yet, great as they were then, and are now, they have
always been only a pace ahead of us, only that vital step
ahead when the end of the Scottish season has arrived. A few

breaks and that could so easily have been altered in our favour. Remember, too, we took three points from them in the league last season. A little more consistency, a little streak of luck in front of goal and we would have been in ahead of them when the season ended. Even in the years of our failure our defence has proved itself the equal of the Celtic defence. Our run in the European Cup Winners' Cup proved that.

Anyhow, the disappointment with Rangers last year was very nearly matched with the disappointment I had with Scotland, disappointment because even after that memorable Wembley victory over England we could not reach the knock-out stages of the European International Championship.

Yet, it was not the World Cup holders who stopped us getting there. Rather it was the genius of one player who kept us from reaching our target, the genius of a player who shares my views of Sir Alf Ramsey's tactics, Georgie Best of Manchester United and Ireland. His genius struck us one October day in Belfast at Windsor Park.

Right through the international season we had an unsettled team because of injuries and suspensions and on that opening day in Belfast it was no different.

We were without Jim Baxter, Billy Bremner and Bobby Lennox. Ireland didn't have these worries. What they had was George Best at his most magnificent. He was in the type of mood when he is completely unstoppable. No player alive would have held him that day and George admitted later that he had his finest-ever game in his home town of Belfast.

Windsor Park has always been a bad ground for Scotland teams. That particular day it was a nightmare with George Best the number one villain, the man responsible for us losing. Then, when we hoped that he might do the same against England at Wembley he was injured and pulled out of the team.

Best is one of that small select group of players whom I
admire more than any others, players who can be described
as ball players, but who still look after themselves. There is
no need to shout for 'protection' for George Best. George has
a toughness in him that makes him get up after even the
fiercest tackles and play on with as much spirit as ever.

The two other players I would put into that category are
Eusebio of Portugal and Pele of Brazil. The Benfica man is
tremendously powerful, very strong and able to shake off the
hardest tackle. I've been most impressed by this ability in the
two games I've played against him.

Pele was exactly the same on the night I came up against
him. Tackling him was like tackling a tank. You could feel
your whole body shaking with the impact yet he was still
there, playing away without seeming to notice.

Then, of course, there's the other side to Pele, too, the side
I saw so clearly the night at Hampden when Scotland played
Brazil just a few weeks before they defended their world title
in England. The side that said more clearly than any words—
'I can look after myself'.

John Prentice was the Scotland boss at the time and he
had given the job of shadowing Pele to Leeds United's Billy
Bremner. Billy did the job well, just too well as far as the
world's greatest player was concerned. Like any other player
Pele did not like being marked closely. Some players put up
with it and simply try to break clear. Some react by trying
to upset the man who has been given the shadow job, and
that was Pele's way.

It happened in the first half when he went up for a high
ball at the edge of our penalty area. Little Billy was behind
him ready to go up when suddenly Pele appeared to draw
back his elbow and connect with Billy's face. Down he went
and there was pandemonium on the park. Few of the fans in

the 80,000 crowd knew what had happened. They saw the two men go up and then Billy was down on the ground. They probably thought there had been a clash of heads. There hadn't. I saw exactly what had happened.

I was just a few yards from the incident and I'll never forget the cold-blooded way that Pele did it. There was no thought of going for the ball, simply the thought of letting Billy know he didn't want any more of his close-marking. I always think of that when I read how Pele doesn't intend to play in the next World Cup because it will be 'too physical' for him.

Still, the Pele incident apart, the match against the Brazilians was one that I enjoyed because it was the first time we had played against a South American team. You learn from these games all the time and meeting South American players adds even more to your soccer education. They have tremendous smoothness of movement, all of them running with the grace of a natural athlete. And their ball control is fantastic. Brazil were a team who reminded me very much of the great Real Madrid side who won the European Cup at Hampden in 1960. A flowing team, with artistry and attacking football their main aim. Maybe that's why the Brazilians lost their world title, for the last World Cup was not the place for attacking football. Of the South American teams who were in England the Argentinians were most likely to succeed because they allied the grace of movement and the individual skills to a ruthlessness that no one else could ever match.

It would be nice to think that I might be playing against some of these teams in the World Cup in Mexico in 1970. Just as nice, possibly, to be playing against them some time for Rangers in a World Club Championship clash after a European Cup victory.

But these are dreams. Not predictions. There will be no predictions from me except for this, that as captain of Rangers I'll be giving every ounce of effort to help the team to a trophy victory. For the club. For the supporters. And most of all for myself so that I can partly wipe out the memories of these last two blank years.